In The Fullness of Time

In The Fullness of Time

The End of the Age May Be Closer Than You Think!

Don Brewer

Advantage®

Published by Advantage, Charleston, South Carolina.
Member of Advantage Media Group.

Printed in the United States of America

ISBN: 978-1-59932-018-2
Library of Congress Control Number: 2007921311

PART I

The Beginning

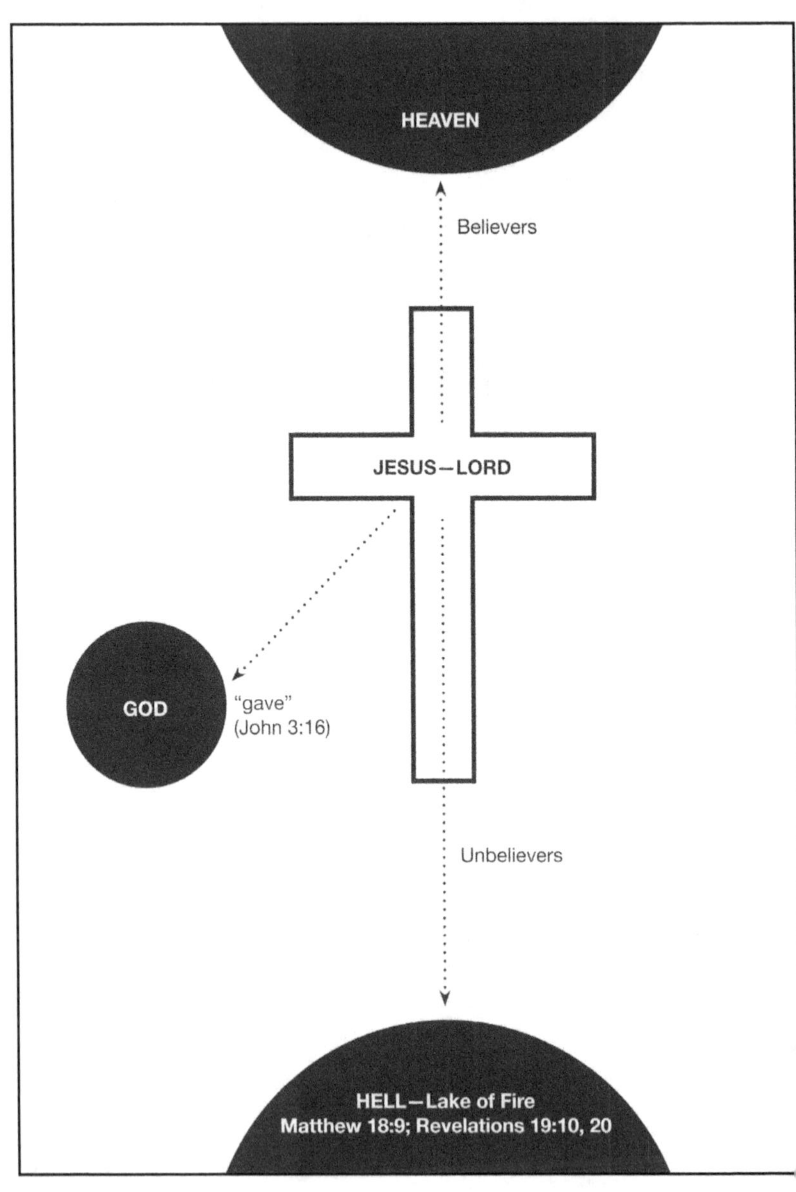
HEAVEN
Believers
JESUS—LORD
GOD
"gave"
(John 3:16)
Unbelievers
HELL—Lake of Fire
Matthew 18:9; Revelations 19:10, 20

THERE WAS A TIME when only the eternal God existed. The word "beginning" as it is used in Genesis 1 and John 1, refers to this time before what we know as time. John says that "in the beginning," refers to the continued existence of something in past time. This means that the Word simply existed. There is reference to a time of creation of the Word, but only to the fact that the Word (Christ) existed. The "Word" in the Greek text is logos which had a significant meaning. Ultimately, it is a description of Christ.

In Genesis 1:1, "the beginning" is not God's beginning, because He always existed, but it is the beginning of God's dealing with His creation. God is the Creator who creates and without God there is no beginning. The Hebrew word for "created" is used only in the Old Testament to refer to the creative activity of God.

When God breathed into Adam, He breathed the life of His Spirit into the vessel made of clay. Thus, man became a living soul.

Man does not only have a body; man is body and soul. To be concerned only about the human body is to lose contact with the power of holiness in the world. If you believe that the body is simply a resting place for the spirit and that the body has no future with God you have to tear out (1 Corinthians 15) from your Bible. The real you is body, soul and spirit, because we are made in his image.

John tells us that "all thing were made by him." He also tells of the creation of the natural world and goes on to describe that the Creator and sustainer of the Universe existed before time began. There was no creation before the logos, no created existence before the logos, and no created essence before the essence of the logos. I know like John, the "logos" (Christ) which is the Word or Creator and Sustainer existed before time began and the Word was divine- "the Word was God." The creation of the universe was accomplish by none other than God.

Christ always comes on time and the earliest prophecy concerning His coming was in the Garden of Eden when God spoke to the serpent following the fall of Adam and Eve. God said to the serpent: "And I will put enmity between thee and the woman, and between thy seed and her seed; it shall bruise thy head, and thou shalt bruise his heel" (Genesis 3:15).

The seed of the woman would be Jesus, who would inflict a mortal wound upon the serpent. It was planned by God that the Redeemer would be the seed of a woman, that is, a man. His life on earth would be for the purpose of bruising the devil, defeating him and establishing the foundation whereby men might be restored to their rightful place with God. While bruising the head of the serpent, His heel would also be bruised. This is a reference to His passion and crucifixion.

Christ is revealed to us whenever we seek Him. It is then we see Him working for us in everything. Each of us needs to discover Christ for themselves and to keep discovering Him. In order for any friendship to grow, we must learn more and more about the other person. Studying, the Book of Revelation is very important, for it is the revelation of Christ.

In the very first chapter of the Revelation we are shown the living Christ as eternal, majestic and sovereign. He is alive and He is in full control. This part that is revealed of Him will give our lives new joy, new peace, and new meaning.

The clouds are his Chariots, He rides on the wings of the wind. The chief theme of Revelation is found in Revelation 1:7: "He cometh with Clouds; and every eye shall see him, and they also which pierced him; and all kindreds of earth shall wail because of him. Even so, amen".

This verse was prophecy in (Daniel 7:13), it was used by John in his message to the early church and this is a picture of Jesus returning with clouds at the ascension of Jesus. In like manner it was said, He would come again. He ascended up into a cloud, and when He returns, He will return with the clouds. We are looking for His glorious return at anytime now, because all signs of His return have been fulfilled. Everyone must be ready, because each individual must seek out his own salvation, in order to be able to come face-to-face with the Creator.

Every Christian will be looking up with a sense of victory, but the evil men will look upon Christ with fear and trembling. They will mourn because they did not accept Him as Savior and Lord. Those who have accepted Christ, must live for Him and look for His coming with clouds.

All the people who have not invited Jesus into their hearts, will have pain and agony, when they see that it was the Creator of the universe, the King of Kings and Lord of Lords, that they have crucified by continuing in sin. All men bound to sin will feel this same torment. As John has it, "all Kindred of the earth shall wail because of him".

God speaks of His eternal nature in Revelation 1:8. HE calls Himself the "Alpha and Omega, the beginning and the end." Alpha and Omega are the beginning and the ending of the Greek alphabet. Everything that man can think of can be found between these two letters. There is nothing missing in God. He is everything we need.

Our God created everything, and no matter how things may look, He is still in control. He is "the beginning and the ending". He created the universe in the beginning and He will be there in the end of all things. He will fulfill all things in the fullness of time.

We all need to know that the whole world is in His hands. Jesus came and broke the chains by which death held us and we became children of life, no longer slaves to Death. In Revelation 1:8 we see God spoken of as He "which is, and which was, and which is to come." HE is a God who is there, and who will always be there for us.

Christ has taken the role as High Priest for us. The writer of Hebrews has it that Jesus "ever liveth to make intercession for them" (Hebrews 7:25). It is Jesus who sits at the right hand of the Father and intercedes in our behalf. He is more fit than anyone else to fill the position of High Priest because, He has experienced trials and tribulations as we have.

He is also a King and King over the whole universe. He has dominion over all of His creation. Jesus is also the messenger of God that was sent to Daniel. So we see, Christ is our intercessor, our ruler, and our messenger. The Book of Revelation is a message brought from God by our High Priest and by our King.

When Christ revealed himself to John, (Revelation 1:17) "he fell at his feet as dead." God said to Moses, "shall no man see me, and live" (Exodus 33:20). The glory of God and of the heavenly Christ causes men to fall before them. The sinner can't look into the face of perfect holiness and the unrighteous can't stand in the presence of righteousness.

Jesus does not want His church to be unrighteous but wants the church to live holy and to strive for perfection. Then and only then can we stand in His presence and not fear. Jesus does not want His church to fear because "fear not" is echoed throughout the Bible. Christ, urges us to leave our fears behind us and keep our eyes on Him.

We need only to fear Him, because He is Ruler of death (Revelation 1:18,19). He will also be our Judge after death. Jesus still lives on and He is the Key to Revelation. God gave Revelation to Jesus then Jesus gave it to the angel and John wrote it down for us. The reason Jesus is the Key to Revelation is found in Revelations 1:18-19. "I am he that liveth and was dead; and, behold, I am alive for evermore, Amen; and have the Keys of hell, and of death. Write the things which thou has seen, and the things which are, and the things which shall be hereafter."

If humankind had obeyed God from the first man Adam on, then the last Adam, Jesus Christ, would not have had to die. "For as in Adam all die, even so in Christ shall all be made alive" (1 Corinthians 15:22).

"For if by one man's offense death reigned by one; much more they which receive abundance of grace and of the gift of righteousness shall reign in life by one, Jesus Christ" (Romans 5:17).

We see in Genesis 1 the first blessings of God to humankind. In Genesis 2:16 we have the first command from God to humankind, "But of the tree of the knowledge of good and evil, thou shalt not eat of it: for in the day that thou eatest thereof thou shalt surely die." Man is not God's slave; he is free to take charge of this world and exercise the ordained dominion and subdue it. The opportunity from God has come as a challenge and a promise. It is the fullest expression of what it truly means to be human.

However, verse 17 contains the only thing Adam was not to do but he had to choose to eat of the tree of knowledge of good and evil or not to eat of this fruit and obey God. God told him to live by the fruit of life that comes through His Word. If Adam decides to gain the knowledge of good and evil, then he decides to replace the Word of God. The Word of God says, "trust the Lord and not lean on our own understanding".

This is not an excuse to be ignorant! Nor is it an excuse to fail in discerning between good and evil! But, it is a word from God that His wisdom and understanding of good and evil are more right than ours will ever be, because all wisdom comes from God. If Adam would have been obedient to God, he would have known life, but Adam wanted to do it his way and will discover the horror of evil, and the fact disobedience to His Word brings eternal death.

Sin not only has an eternal debt to pay but while we are on this earth. Adam's sin price was great, plus he had shame and fear. In Genesis 3:8-10 the hiding and fear of God are related to being naked before God. The effect of sin is when Adam hid himself, which results in him being guilty before God.

Here is mankind, who has just opened the doors of damnation upon human life thinking that he could be all wise, huddling together in shame and fear in the trees, listening to the steps of an all wise God walking in the garden. The cool of the day "implies the evening when man's work is done and God would join him for times of fellowship. This was why God created man in the first place, and is a wonderful picture of the fellowship Adam and Eve had with God prior to their sin.

Adam has not rejected Eve but blamed her for their trouble. She is still his wife, just as God had planned, man and woman to be joined together. They still need each other and cannot exist separately, because God created man and woman to co-exist together; but now they need each other in shame, blame and fear. The holy fellowship they had with each other and with God has now been divided; yet, they are still together.

Adam and Eve's home is not the same since they disobeyed God and sinned. Instead, given the opportunity to repent, the man betrays the woman. She had led him into temptation; now he seeks to leave her betrayed.

In Genesis 3:12, Adam says "and the man said the woman whom thou gavest to be with me, she gave me of the tree, and I did eat." Adam first blamed God in the first clause of the above verse, "The woman whom thou gavest to be with me."

God knew it wasn't good for man to be given a man to live with and also knew it wasn't good for man to be a bachelor. God gave to Adam the best he had to offer, which was a woman but Adam blamed the woman for both of their sins, in the second clause of verse 12, "she gave me of the tree, and I did eat."

The woman in verse 13 shifts her blame to the serpent and accuses him of beguiling her. What Adam and Eve failed to see is God's grace and mercy. If only they would have repented and told the truth to God, their sins would have been forgiven, because He is the same yesterday, today and forever. Their first sin of eating the forbidden fruit but failing to repent has cut short a clear revelation of grace.

The serpent is cursed in verse 14 but God has not damned humankind. There is mercy here, free for the asking. There was judgment when they sinned and there is judgment now when we sin. The only difference between the two is, they will pay for their sin, but they will not be cursed by God. Sin is cursed, but not the person! Christ took our curse on the cross, when He shed His precious blood for our sins.

The woman's punishment is directed at the source of her life: childbearing and her husband. What was meant to be a source of great joy, childbearing is turned into a place of pain and sorrow.

The punishment also changes the relationship between the woman and man. She tempted him and he betrayed her, and now their quality of life is affected. "Her desire is for her husband and he shall exercise rule over her," God said. Many modern feminists are offended by this passage. God knew best and gave the woman a measure of grace here. What God actually says, is her desire would be for her own husband, and no other; and only her husband, not another, shall rule over her.

Eve is now, mother of all living. The woman remains as the source of earthly life, (verse 20) "and Adam called his wife's name Eve; because she was the mother of all living." In verse 23 and 24 the man and woman are driven from the Garden of Eden and left on their own. God desired obedience but they chose isolation when He had desired community and fellowship.

I'm so glad there was another garden, and there Christ was willing to give His life as a ransom for every soul on earth however; a salvation that is through faith can be rejected. But it was still provided "unto all men." God's Word says, "as by the offense of one judgment came upon all men to condemnation; Even so by the righteousness of one the free gift came upon all men unto justification of life" (Romans 5:18). I praise God, for His unspeakable gift, which He gave free to all who receive Him.

The writer of Hebrews 1:1-13 draws a contrast between Jesus and the Prophets. He said, He "spoke in time past unto the fathers by the Prophets," but now God speaks through His own Son. Prophets were the friends of God and were used by God, but Jesus was His Son. The Prophets grasped part of the mind of God; but Jesus was the mind of God.

Jesus continued and fulfilled the Old Testament and in the fullness of time consummated or fulfilled it. His word is the final authority, and that word has come to us in the person of His Son, who speaks to us today.

The writer of Hebrews also said, Jesus sustains all the things by His powerful words. John shared that same thought when he wrote: "Thou art worthy, O Lord, thou hast created all things, and for thy pleasure they are and were created" (Revelations 4:11). Paul also wrote: "all things were created by him: And he is before all things. And by him all things consist" (Colossians 1:15,16).

Jesus is described as the express image or exact representation of the Father in (Hebrews 1:3,4), "Who being the brightness of his glory, and the express image of his person, and upholding all things by the word of his power, when he had by himself purged our sins, sat down on the right hand of the Majesty on high; Being made so much better than the angels, as He hath by inheritance obtained a more excellent name than they." He is exactly like the Father.

Having completed His earthly mission, He returned to His Father, and now sits at the Father's right hand, making intercession for His children. He now pleads the cases brought to Him in prayer and presents their prayers to the Father.

The writer of (Hebrews 1:4) is saying there is one who is "much better" or superior to the angels, even Jesus Christ, the Son of God. No angel has ever occupied such a position, because it was reserved for the Son of God. Jesus occupies this position beside God because He is far superior to all prophets, to all angels and all creation, because He is their Creator.

Christ's position beside the Father is as an intercessor, and He is our one greatest source of help in everyday life. We have everything to make us complete in Him. Paul says, "For in him dwelleth all the fullness of the Godhead bodily. And ye are completed in him" (Colossians 2:9,10). The Father and the Son are each an essential part of the completeness of the relationship. Jesus said, "I and my Father are one" (John 10:30).

The coming King Jesus, and according to scripture His coming is soon. He will reign forever on His everlasting throne, according to Psalms 45:6, "Thy throne, O God, is forever and ever: the sceptre of thy Kingdom is a right sceptre." Also in Hebrews 1:8 he says, "But unto the Son he saith, Thy throne, O God, is forever and ever: the sceptre of righteousness is the sceptre of thy kingdom." The scepter is a staff held by kings, and is the sign of their sovereignty or authority. Verse 13 means any king able to put his foot on conquered land or enemies neck in Old Testament times, meant absolute master.

According to Hebrews 1:10, the Father gives credit for the creation to Christ. He laid the foundations of the earth. The heavens are the work of His hands. Christ, is one to whom all creative acts are ascribed, so faith in Him promises an unending life and enough grace through His great and mighty power. He is our source of power and hope.

In Hebrews 1:11,12, the Father says, "They shall perish; but thou remains; and they shall wax as old as doth a garment; And as a vesture shalt thou fold them up, and they shall be changed: but thou art the same, and thy years shall not fail."

The father says, that the things which Christ created perish, but that He would remain. He likened the fading of created things to the wearing out of clothes. You wear a new dress or suit, and it will eventually be worn out or thrown away. But God said, it is not that way with the Son. He is the same yesterday, today and forever.

The Holy Spirit was with the Father and Son in the beginning when "God said, Let us make man in our image, after our likeness." The dispensation of the Holy Spirit began when Jesus was crucified, resurrected, and returned to His Father. The Holy Spirit began His work on earth, on the day of Pentecost, "and they were all filled with the Holy Ghost, and began to speak with tongues, as the Spirit gave them utterance" (Acts 2:4).

The Prophet said in Joel 2:28,29 that God would pour out His "Spirit" upon all nations. The fulfillment of Joel's prophecy was made clear by the apostle Peter when he said in Acts 2:16,17,18, "But this is that which was spoken by the prophet Joel: it shall come to pass in the last days, saith God, I will pour out my Spirit upon all flesh: and your sons and your daughters shall prophecy, and your young men shall see visions, and your old men shall dream dreams: and on my servants and on my handmaidens I will pour out in those days of my Spirit and they shall prophecy."

Peter made it clear that this promise was fulfilled on the Day of Pentecost. Peter referred them back to their own Prophet Joel. The Prophet was speaking of a time when The Spirit would not only work through judges, prophets and Kings, but would be shared by all God's people, in every nation on earth.

In the service after the infilling, three thousand souls were born into the Kingdom of God. The message demonstrated the importance of being filled with the Spirit. His coming makes us happy but His coming is not primarily to make us happy or to make us Holy, but to make us useful in His Kingdom. We should have been made happy and holy in regeneration and sanctification. The Holy Spirit seeks to make us effective in witnessing and in ministry as a whole. Every believer should seek to be filled after they are saved and sanctified.

Joel's prophecy was set to be fulfilled in the last days. The last days began with Christ's first advent and will end with His second advent. Jesus prayed to the Father when He reached the throne after His resurrection, that He would send us someone to comfort, help and lead us.

The last days for the Holy Spirit and this dispensation to work in man will end when He raptures the church. According to the signs He gave to us His coming is very close at hand. Peter declared that the outpouring of the Holy Spirit was proof that Jesus had assumed His position beside the Father and had already asked the Father's "Spirit" to be poured out. Personally receiving the Holy Spirit is proof that Jesus is sitting beside the Father.

The reason Peter knew this was "that" was the fulfillment of prophecy which he spoke about in Acts 2:16. "But this is that which was spoken by the prophet Joel".

God told us things that would happen in the future which we find in the Old Testament and which are fulfilled in the New Testament. Judas was that "familiar friend" which "He trusted" who betrayed Jesus and this is found in

Psalms 41:9. Judas was a bad example but the Bible teaches that good will triumph over evil in the end, however history records many instances where evil has triumphed. Satan wins a few battles but God always wins the war. The Garden of Eden is another place where evil won, but in the fullness of time the Lord will prevail. The victory will be His.

Jesus will be on time for His victory, because He has always been on time and everything from creation has happened when He said, it would. The coming of the Messiah was the desire of all nations (Haggai 2:7) and the hope of Israel (Acts 28:20). From Genesis to Malachi the focus was on the nature of the Savior and the fullness of time of His coming.

Leaders like Joshua, became a type of the great "Captain of our salvation" (Hebrews 2:10); every prophet, a type of the "teacher come from God" (John 3:2); Kings like David a type of "the King of Glory" (Psalms 24:7-18); every sufferer, like Jeremiah or Job, a type of the "man of sorrows" (Isaiah 53:3).

Isaiah's prophecy was written more than 700 years before His coming (7:14). His family origin (11:1), His anointing with the Holy Spirit (11:2; 42:1), His ministry (42:7; 49:6; 61:1-3), His rejection by the Jews (53:3), His silence by His accusers (53:7), His burial in a rich man's tomb (53:9), which was fulfilled in Matthew 27:59 & 60, His victory over death Isaiah 53:10-12, which was fulfilled in Matthew 28:5-8.

The fulfilled prophecies of Jesus Christ's coming as the Messiah, demonstrates that all Bible prophecies will be fulfilled in God's time. Jesus will always come on time because

He always seeks the Father's will and not His own will.

God is love and He seeks to love us and care for us eternally. The eternity of God and His eternal care for us does not mean that God is not aware of who we are. God knows every circumstance of our lives. The Psalmist, David, begins by "crying" out unto the Lord. He gives reasons for the plea in Psalms 102: 3-11. He lists time as one of the reasons for His plea. Human futility in comparison to time is described, "My days are consumed and my days are like a shadow that declineth," depict the demands of time. He later recognizes how great God is in relationship to time. In Psalms 102:16-22, God's care for the people of God is described.

In Psalms 102:23-24 the Psalmist recognizes God's care for him personally. The Psalmist refers to the time in his own life when he cried out in "the midst of his days." He then recognized God's control of time when he says, "Thy years are throughout all generations; of old hast thou laid the foundations of the earth."

He realized that God's eternal power and control of time is used for God's care of him. In Psalm 102:28, he praises God for the care of the "children of thy servants." God's eternal care will be "continued and established."

The reason God knows how to care for His children is that He is omniscient which means "all-knowing" (Psalms 139:1-6). God knows everything that has ever been and everything that will ever be. In describing God's omniscience, David refers to God's infinite knowledge of Him. David says in Psalm 139:1 that he has searched him and known him. Verse 2 describes God knowing David's "down setting and uprising." God is aware of what David does with his time, during his leisure and his work. He also is aware of what we do with our time. God also knew what David's thoughts were, when He said though "afar off" God also knows what we are thinking about. Distance or time means nothing to our God.

In verse 3, David testifies of God's "compassing my path," And God is aware "with all my ways." In verse 4 David says that God knows every word that he speaks. This emphasis is shown in the fact God knows his words "altogether." There are many facets to our spoken communication that are not spoken. Gestures, intentions, and emotions are all part of the words that we speak.

God's omniscience is aware of all that is involved in our communication. God understands our thoughts, our words, and even what our intentions are. We may outwit and fool man but we can't fool God.

Verses 5 and 6 of Psalm 139 says, "Thou hast beset behind and before and laid thine hand upon me. Such knowledge is too wonderful for me; it is high, I can not attain unto it."

God's omniscience protects David's past and his future. God's ability to know all means that God cares for David in an all-knowing way, but his care is personal. David says God "laid His hand upon him." The word "Hand" here means personal care.

God is always with us. He is omnipresent which means that God is present everywhere. There is no place where He is not present. The presence of God is almighty to the extent that it extends into all space at all times. In Psalm 139:7-12, David has given descriptions of God's omnipresence. David lists places where God is such as: "heaven." God is there; "hell" God is also there. He was in the fire with the three Hebrew boys when they did not burn. God is there, and David recognizes that God's omnipresence means that God is not only present, but He is also personally ministering with His ever-present "hand."

The personal care of the Lord, makes "the darkness to shine." David does not deny the existence of the darkness. His frustration, confusion, and depression, is real. However, God, who is ever present to minister, causes the despair of human existence to shine by the light of His love. God is no respecter of persons, and he will make "the darkness to shine" for each of us because of His personal care. He is always personally ministering with his ever-present "hand."

The word omnipotent means all-powerful. Specifically omnipotence means the power of God to execute His will. In Jeremiah 32, He reflects on the fact that God is the Creator of Heaven and the earth, the natural life which is all creatures and spiritual life represented by man, who were made in His image.

THE PROMISE

I see you standing there,
And your hurt I can not bear.

I see the despair in you're eyes,
As you try to cover the lies.

I see what could have come,
If I didn't send my Son.

To show you the way,
To where the lion and sheep lay.

To where there will be no more sickness and tears,
And we shall rejoice all the years.

Where you will live for eternity,
As long as you put your faith in me.

You might not see my plan as clear today,
But listen to me when I say;

That you are a child of mine,
And you will never be left behind,

And you will see the paths paved with gold.
And you will believe everything that you've been told,

You will feel the love fill your heart,
As you enter a new beginning a new start.

Shelby Marie Taylor, 2005.

The omnipotence of God in Jeremiah 32: 18, 19 displays God's love and care for His people. The omnipotence of God is not so powerful that he does not provide care for this natural world. God is all-powerful in order that His will may be accomplished.

Creator of the heaven and the earth. It is by God's great power that heaven and earth was created. Jeremiah says, "There is nothing too hard for thee." Nothing is too wonderful or impossible for God. Jeremiah knows this and declares it in prayer, when he was wanting to do God's will in purchasing some land.

Jeremiah says God shows "loving kindness unto thousands, and there is nothing too hard for Him." God's will is just and is maintained by His power. In Jeremiah 32:19 Jeremiah says, God is mighty because "thine eyes are open upon all the ways of the sins of men: to give everyone according to his ways according to the fruit of His doings." God's justice is the reason He shows His might. When we pray as Jeremiah did in verses 17-19, it's a good thing to know that we have the support of the omnipotent God!

God wanted to be Israel's King but man compromised by being lead by Priests, Prophets and Judges until about 400 years after the Old Testament period had ended, which told of the birth, life, death and resurrection of Jesus. Over 100 prophecies were fulfilled by Christ, who fulfilled all of the Old Testament prophecies in the fullness of time, when his son will be King of Kings and Lord of Lords.

Included in those prophecies was that the seed of woman (Eve) would bruise the head of Satan. When Jesus died on the cross for the sins of the world, the Old Testament system of sacrifice was no longer needed. Jesus opened up the way of salvation by grace through faith in Jesus Christ the Son of God.

PART II

Christ was Born

GOD ALWAYS GIVES US A SIGN and in his time His prophecy will be fulfilled. About 700 years before Christ was born, God gave His prophet Isaiah a sign of how He could be with us, referring to the human nature of Christ. In Isaiah 7:14 he said, "therefore the Lord himself shall give you a sign; Behold, a virgin shall conceive, and bear a son, and shall call His name Immanuel." He used the word behold to show that it was a great event. A virgin would conceive, not by the ordinary course of nature, but by the influence of the Holy Spirit (Matthew 1:18-25).

The apostle Paul said, "God was manifest in the flesh" (1 Timothy 3:16). When the Prophet said a virgin was going to bear a son, he also said, she would name Him Immanuel, meaning "God with us" This was contrary to custom. The father was always given the right of giving the child its name. But here that responsibility was given to the mother.

Therefore, this Son was to be conceived in such a way as not to have an earthly father. He was, therefore, to be called "God with us." Immanuel, a name that could not be given to a man that was not God. This name means He was to be the Son of God, clothed with our flesh, and taking onto Himself our nature. Immanuel was a title of excellence and authority that He would possess above all others. He was not just a human being. He was also the God-man who accepted the role of humanity and became one of us that

He might save all who believe on Him and accept Him, as the way from earth to Heaven. In the announcement of His birth, (Luke 1:26-36) an angel in (Luke 1:3), said, "that holy thing which shall be born of thee shall be called the Son of God."

The Holy Ghost revealed to Simeon, that he wouldn't see death before he had seen "the Lord's Christ" (Luke 2:26).

In the Book of Micah, Christ's birth was foretold, along with His kingdom and conquest of the antichrist. In Micah 5:1 Christ will not only judge Israel but of all men. In verse 2, Micah tells us that the ruler of Israel would be born in the little town of Bethlehem which was fulfilled in Matthew 2:11.

At the end of the book of Micah, the prophet tells us that as man He had a beginning but as God He has always been.

In Matthew 1:20, the angel of the Lord appeared to Joseph in a dream saying, "Joseph, thou son of David, fear not to take unto thee Mary thy wife." In Matthew 1:21 he said, "and she shall bring forth a son, and thou shalt call his name Jesus: for he shall save his people from their sins." This was to fulfill the prophecy of Isaiah (7:14)

Joseph brought the baby Jesus to the Temple on the eighth day of life, the Holy Spirit drew Simeon to the Temple where he took the baby in his arms and declared He was the promised Christ (Luke 2:21-35). When Christ was baptized a voice from heaven declared: "This is my beloved Son" (Matthew 3:17).

Later Peter confessed that Jesus is the Son of God (Matthew 16:16). Jesus was a Jew by earthly birth. He had an earthly mother and a Heavenly Father. He lived within the jurisdiction of Palestine, except for a short time in Egypt. His ministry took place within a fifty mile radius, which is an extremely small area in comparison to the worldwide impact of Jesus ministry and message.

One record of Jesus' birth is found in Matthew 2:1-33, and the other was verified by Doctor Luke. The genealogy in Luke seems to follow the Davidic line through Mary, the mother of Jesus. The genealogy in Matthew seems to trace the earthly ancestry through Joseph, the earthly father of Jesus.

I'm so glad that Joseph obeyed the Lord in Matthew 2:13-23, when he took Jesus and Mary into Egypt and remained there until it was safe to leave. I'm also so glad that the wise men knew how to follow God's plan in Matthew 2:12. God revealed to the Wise Men that they should shun Herod and return to the East in a way different from that which they had come. God wanted to preserve His Son's life and allow Him to fulfill His purpose and this was to give us peace and make us friends again with God.

Jesus gave us peace and made us friends again with God, and now we are justified or declared guiltless and blameless before God. In Romans 5:2 Jesus is the access or door "by faith into this grace wherein we stand and rejoice," or boast in "hope of the glory of God." The psalmist wrote, "God judgeth the righteous, and God is angry with the wicked everyday" (Psalm 7:11). While God loves the sinner and strives to win him from its hold, He is angered by sin and His wrath is set against it.

Through Jesus, God is at peace with us. Our hope of acceptance rests not upon our imperfect conformity to the laws of God, but to the faith we have in the Lord Jesus Christ.

We are indebted to Christ for peace with God, and through Him we have access into the grace because he is the door to God. Paul said, "For through him (Jesus) we both have access by one Spirit unto the Father" (Ephesians 2:18). He also said," In whom we have boldness and access with confidence by the faith of him" (Ephesians 3:12).

The assurance of our future produces a joyful spirit because that blessed hope recognizes a present possession. Peace, stability, and hope are the by-products of justification by faith. Paul says, "Hope maketh not ashamed; because the love of God is shed abroad in our hearts by the Holy Ghost which is given unto us" (Romans 5:5). "Shed abroad in our hearts by the Holy Ghost," means poured into our hearts by the Holy Ghost and by the grace of God in Christ.

Grace Abuse

In this day that we're living in,
We hear of people being abused time and time again.
And as we read the newspaper it seems like every day,
We hear of a little child being beaten or mistreated in some way.
And we can turn the pages only to find,
More and more abuse's of this kind.

Yes the headline's usually tells of someone taking another's life,
Or maybe of a husband who battered his wife.

Or even of a junky who felt he couldn't cope,
And murdered to get some money to buy a little dope.

Yes in this day we're living in I'm sure we're bound to hear.
Of innocent life's being taken while someone drives after drinking too much beer.
Yes the paper's are full of people abusing their selves and each other,
Of parent's hating their children of children hating their father and mother.

But of all the abuse's that have ever taken place,
The worst of all is when we abuse God's grace.
You see God has made a way for us to be free from this world of wickedness and sin,
But we abuse his grace by not letting him in.

And I'm sure if we could hear the soul's in hell and listen to what they have to say,
They would tell us of how they abused God's grace day after day.
Yes many could probably tell of how God's spirit once dealt with them but they
refused him with all their might,
And kept saying in their heart I'll serve you one day Lord when the time is right.
But right now I'm having too much fun doing the things that I want to do,
But one day Lord I really plan to serve you.
They'd probably go on by saying boy Satan really deceived me,
'Cause I thought I could serve God when I got ready you see.

But I kept choosing to live a life of sin
Not knowing time for me would soon end.
And now I'm warning you not to come to this awful place,
By rejecting and abusing this marvelous thing called grace!!!

Vanessa Taylor, October, 1984

PART III

CHRIST THE REDEEMER & SAVIOR

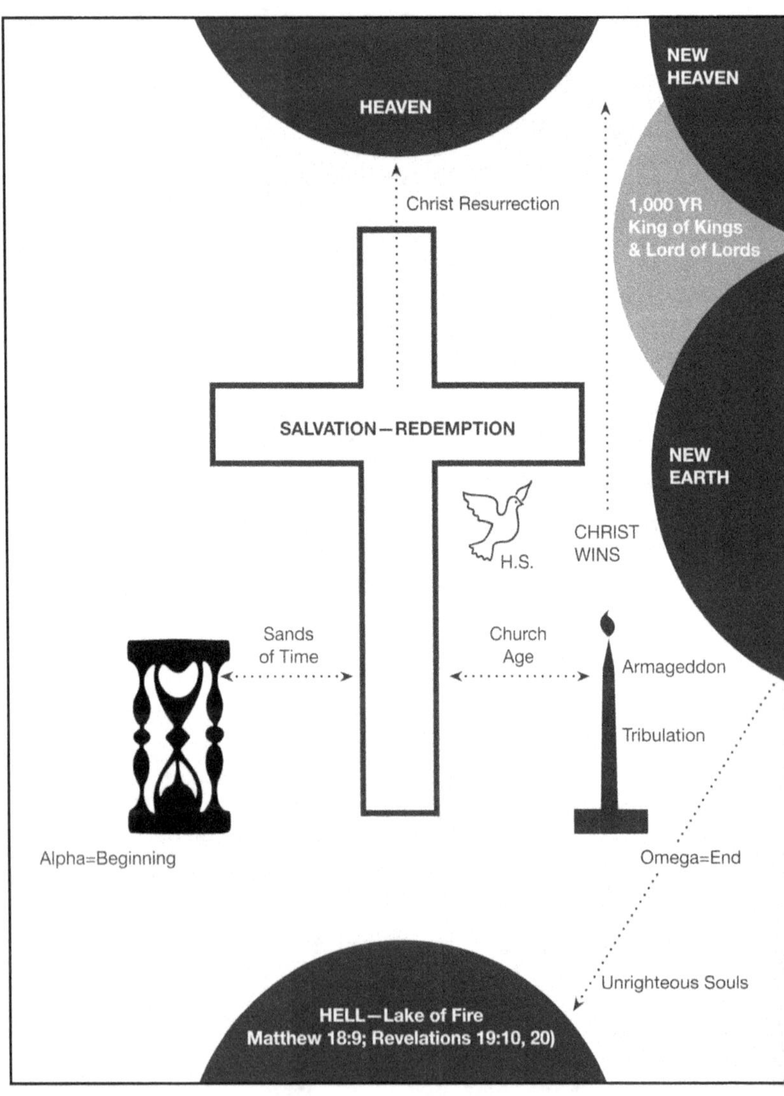
HEAVEN
NEW
HEAVEN
Christ Resurrection
1,000 YR
King of Kings
& Lord of Lords
SALVATION—REDEMPTION
NEW
EARTH
H.S.
CHRIST
WINS
Sands
of Time
Church
Age
Armageddon
Tribulation
Alpha=Beginning
Omega=End
Unrighteous Souls
HELL—Lake of Fire
Matthew 18:9; Revelations 19:10, 20)

BEFORE THE MESSIAH COULD COME, the world had to be prepared for Him. The following events had to happen: The dispersing of the Jews, with their law and prophecies, throughout the Roman Empire; the establishment of a world empire, thus spreading the gospel easier; the almost universal use of the Greek language; and the failure of the Pagan religions and philosophies to meet the needs of humanity. God had prepared the world for the coming of His Son; and in the fullness of time, He sent him forth.

God's new creation wrought through redemption helps fulfill His original purpose for man and all creation. We all know of the "beginnings." The universe (Genesis 1), mankind (Genesis 2), sin (Genesis 3), suffering (Genesis 3), the beginnings of God's redemption program (Genesis 3), the beginning of civilization (Genesis 4), and the beginnings of the Hebrew nation (Genesis 12). God is the uncreated, Eternal, Everlasting, the always, was, and always will be God. God the Son was with His Father, the uncreated Creator when "in the beginning God created." The proof of this in scripture is found in Genesis 1:26.

God spoke first through nature, then through dreams and visions, through the law, and through the prophets. Finally God spoke to people face-to-face by His Son. All things began with Christ and all things will end with Christ (Revelation 22:13).

Jesus Christ had two natures; He was man and He was God. As an ancient creed expressed it, "two whole and perfect natures, that is to say, the God, head and manhood, were joined together in one person, never to be divided whereof is one Christ, very God and perfect man".

In the fullness of time Jesus came to redeem everybody from sin. (Galatians 4:4,5) says, "when the fullness of time was come, God sent forth His Son, made of a woman, made under the law, that we might receive the adoption of sons." The Jews had wanted many years for the coming of their Messiah. He was rich, yet for our sakes, He became poor. He became a pauper on this earth that we might be made rich in Him.

Many people in this world thinks Jesus came to make us prosper by giving us money, however He gives us love, joy and peace that the rich can not purchase with money.

Money would not have saved the adulterous woman in John 8:11 but "grace and truth" and mercy flowed out to the woman that Jesus forgave, and He said," neither do I condemn thee: go, and sin no more." These same words were spoken to all born-again believers. For we, like the woman, deserved death, but he showed mercy and we became heirs and joint heirs with Him. With His mercy and grace He still commands us to "Go and sin no more." Jesus did not say that he did not condemn adultery as a sin. He forgave her just like he had done others who had sinned. He just told her to sin no more, proving He did condemn adultery as a sin but that Christ delivered this adulterous woman and many other sinners were redeemed as well.

"And the scribes and Pharisees brought unto him a woman taken in adultery" (John 8:3). And the next verses say, she was caught in the very act of adultery and "the law of Moses commanded us, that such should be stoned: but what sayest thou? Jesus Christ replies, "He that is without sin among you, let him first cast a stone at her" (verse 7). Jesus upheld the law of Moses, but convicted the proud accuses of being themselves worthy of condemnation; the Pharisees withdrew. Jesus teaches us that only the man who himself is without fault has the right to bring judgment on the fault of others. He said, "judge not, that you be not judged. For with what judgment you judge, you shall be judged: and with what measure you mete, it shall be measured to you again. And why beholdest thou the mote that is in thy brother's eye, but considerest not the beam that is in thine own eye?" (Matthew 7:1-3). The difference between Jesus and the scribes and Pharisees was that they wished to condemn; He wished to forgive. Jesus showed love but they chose self-righteousness.

As a Roman tax collector, he would stoop to all sorts of wickedness, to get money. He was regarded as a henchman for Rome. So we know Zacchaeus was deeply despised, a man everybody hated. Not only was Zacchaeus a publican, but he was also the Chief among the publicans. Crookedest crook of all the Crooks! Zacchaeus was rich with houses and lands but his soul was starved because he loved God little and cared not for man that was in distress.

Jesus was passing through Jericho (Luke 19:1). Zacchaeus was little of stature-physically and could not see Jesus because of the crowd (Luke 19:3). So he ran on ahead of the crowd and climbed up into a sycamore tree. When Christ looked up and calls Zacchaeus by name, telling him to come down from the tree (Luke 19:5). This call to Zacchaeus was like the call at the tomb of Lazarus, it was a personal call. At the tomb of Lazarus, Jesus did not call for all the dead to come forth, and at the sycamore tree there were probably a dozen people in the tree, but he singled out Zacchaeus and called him by name. Zacchaeus obeyed the Lord's command and received Christ into his house. The important thing was he "received Christ joyfully."

When Jesus comes into the heart, He comes to put away all sin. Whenever Christ is received, all the guilt of the past is put in the sea of forgetfulness as far as Christ is concerned. While Christ ate the bread from Zacchaeus' table. He fed him the bread of heaven, causing him to hunger and thirst after righteousness. In Luke 19:8, Zacchaeus said that he was going to give half of his goods to the poor. Zacchaeus said he was going to repay fourfold any amount he had taken falsely. He was his own judge and gave himself the sentence of 400 percent. Then after all that, Zacchaeus was giving half his wealth to the poor. The rich, young ruler went away from Jesus sorrowfully. Zacchaeus went the Jesus way happily. Salvation came to Zacchaeus immediately, when he obeyed the Master.

When the people arrived for the Passover feast, Jews were there from all parts of the world to celebrate the fast. In fact the Jews came to Jerusalem for the celebration of all holy days, such as the Feast of Pentecost (Acts 2:5-11).

Word raced through the city that Jesus was coming and the fame of Jesus and His wondrous works caused the people to want to welcome Him. The people broke palm branches from trees that lined His path and waved fronds in joy of his arrival. The people welcomed Jesus with the word "Hosanna", (John 12:13), which means "I entreat you to save me" or "I ask for salvation".

They declared Him to be the King of Israel, one who had come in the name of the Lord. This means that they fully accepted Him to be the Messiah of God. This joyous occasion that Jesus was King of Israel, the one sent of the Father, did not escape the attention of the Pharisees and other enemies of Christ. The crowd were not intimidated by the disbelief of their religious leaders because they recognized Christ as having greater authority than their Jewish leaders. Jesus could easily have claimed His Kingship at that time, but the fullness of time for this to happen had not arrived. The people would have supported Him in gaining the throne but Christ wanted to fulfill all prophecy and do the perfect will of His Father. Christ needed to fulfill all prophecy such as in Psalm 118:19,20 and John 12: 14-16.

The gates mentioned in these verses refer to the gates of Jerusalem, even the gate of the Temple itself. The Jews had expected their Messiah to come with great military and political power and get rid of all of Israel's enemies. He came in peace and righteousness, to establish a spiritual kingdom. Israel as a nation rejected the Messiah, who is the chief cornerstone of all salvation.

The Lord entered Jerusalem riding upon an ass to show His humility and not His military might which they expected. "Fear not, daughter of Zion: behold, thy King cometh, sitting upon an ass's colt" (John 12: 15), is a prophecy of Zechariah 9:9, which says, "Rejoice greatly, O daughter of Zion; shout, O daughter of Jerusalem: behold thy King cometh unto thee: he is just, and having salvation; lowly, and riding upon an ass, and upon a colt the foal of an ass."

"Much people of the Jews therefore knew that he was there; and they came not for Jesus sake only, but that they might see Lazarus also, whom he had raised from the dead" (John 12:9). "Then gathered the chief priests and the Pharisees a council and said, What do we? for this man doeth many miracles" (John 11:47). "Then from that day forth they took counsel together for to put him to death" (John 11:53).

For these men thought if he had power to raise the dead to life again, then he himself, must be put to death. It was tragic that Jesus should be received in Jerusalem with such mixed emotions. The people of Israel received him with rejoicing, calling upon Him for salvation, while the religious leaders received Him as their enemy.

One group would make Jesus King, the other would put Him to death. The first chapter of John says, "He came unto his own, and his own received him not, But as many as received him, to them gave he power to become the sons of God, even to them that believe on his name". I am so glad that I believed on His name and received Him.

No one can imagine that pain that Christ suffered even before He reached the cross. He suffered betrayal at the hands of one of His best friends; denial by a second of His apostles; the weight of the whole world's sins; an illegal arrest, while

He was praying to is Holy Father; a mock trial before his enemies; a parade of false witnesses who spoke against him; and humiliation treatment by the Roman soldiers.

After the trial by the Jews, Jesus had been delivered into the hands of the Romans. He was scourged by them, which means that He was whipped with a big leather whip with a very strong man doing the whipping. The scourge tore and cut the flesh, leaving his flesh in strings like ribbons. Then the soldiers stripped the clothing from Jesus and placed a scarlet robe around Him; this was done in mockery because it was said, that He was a King. The soldiers twisted branches of thorns into a circle and pressed this upon His head like a crown. They bowed before Him and mocked Him, calling Him King of the Jews and Later beat the thorns into His head, with His precious blood running down His face.

The soldiers were merely having fun in their brutal way. They were simply making sport at His painful expense. They spit upon Him and slapped Him across the head with such treatment that would have been inhumane toward even a beast. Jesus suffered all this without trying to defend Himself because this was part of the full price of death He had to pay. After all this cruel treatment, He was led away to the cross.

After leaving the Roman judgment hall, Christ was taken to a small hill outside Jerusalem called Golgotha. The meaning of the word is "a place of the skull." I have been there and have walked inside the empty tomb. The hill, with caves in its side, looks just like a skull. Others believe that it was called Golgotha because it was used as a place of execution.

Jesus was made to carry His cross from the judgment hall to the place of execution. Jesus collapsed under the weight of the cross and Simon was compelled to bear the cross for Christ (Matthew 27:32).

The Romans gave the victims a stupefying drink to help deaden their awareness of the terrible pain to follow. This drink was made from Vinegar, gall, wine and myrrh (Mark 15:23). Jesus refused to drink the "sour wine," and chose rather to feel the full pain of dying.

He did not die unwillingly. He himself said in John 10:17,18: "I lay down my life, that I might take it again. No man taketh it from me, but I lay it down, of myself. I have power to lay it down, and I have power to take it again."

In Romans 5:6-8, Paul calls our attention to the death of the Son of God, when he says, "in due time Christ died for the ungodly." I love verse 8, which says, "But God commendeth His love toward us in that, while we were yet sinners, Christ died for us." Out of Christ's death and resurrection came the power to change lives and to save people from their sins. Out of the death of Jesus came life for all who will believe upon Him. Life springs out of death in God's world and hate turns to love. Just like the seed dies and then we can have the golden sheeves later waving in the wind.

Very rarely will anyone die for a righteous man. But we were ungodly sinners and enemies, yet Christ died for us. God sure showed His love by giving His Son to die for us while we were still sinners. God sent His Son, not to a glorious paradise, but to a disordered planet of sin and sorrow. Then He gave Jesus up to death. His resurrection is a guarantee that all men die a physical death but will live eternally. Jesus in his resurrected body was real to the disciples; though glorified. Reproduced grains are just as real, tangible and material as those sown. God made Christ a sin-offering, that "we might be made the righteousness of God in Him" (2 Corinthians 5:21).

I am sure glad that Christ paid our debt for sin because this is the only way a person can be redeemed is by his faith in Christ, which is our substitute. By our faith in Him, our penalty has been paid and we are counted righteous or justified in God's sight. Christ knew there was no other way that man could be redeemed, when He prayed in the Garden for His Father's will and not His will to be done.

We know that by the sin of Adam all men became sinners and were alienated from God, but through the righteousness of Jesus Christ righteousness is available to everyone on this planet. Through Christ anyone can be restored and be right with God. The apostle Paul says, "For since by man came death, by man came also the resurrection of the dead. For as in Adam all die, even so in Christ shall all be made alive." All mankind actually sinned in Adam so we all need to be made alive. One man's righteousness gave man this "free gift" because Paul says, "But not as the offence, so also is the free gift. For if through the offence of one many be dead, much more the grace of God, and the gift by grace, which is by one man, Jesus Christ, hath abounded unto many" (Romans 5:15).

All men need to be redeemed, because not only have they all sinned, but also have been sinful beings from their beginning. This ought not to be so because God never intended this for His people. Man is faced with his own nature, man knows nothing but sin and self-despair apart from Christ. But in Christ and by the grace of God, man has acceptance, peace, holiness, and power. In Christ we have life and answers to our problems of life.

Paul makes it clear that grace is greater than all our sins. He gives grace freely to all men who believe in Jesus Christ. Any man can partake of this grace, and thereby accept Jesus Christ as Savior. This gift is free to "whosoever will" come. When you come and receive this gift from Christ, which is the grace of God, then the believer becomes a child of God. There is given to him a new life; and this new life's nature make him to want to do the will of God. God loved us so much that He sent His only begotten Son to give us the opportunity to serve Him. The matter is settled once and for all when we accept and obey His Son Jesus Christ.

Redemption by definition denotes deliverance. It might be a physical deliverance such as when God rescued the Hebrews from Egyptian bondage. Or it could be a spiritual deliverance such as occurs in the process of salvation. In the Old Testament, the sacrificial system provided redemption from sin. But in the New Testament, Christ is our Redeemer.

Peter reminded his audience of God' redemption (1 Peter 17-19) when he referred to the Old Testament concept. However, there were some contrasts. First, God now offers redemption to all (verse 17). This means that all of us will be judged by the same standards. Second, our spiritual redemption can't be bought with coins or precious metals (verse 18). No matter how wealthy a person is, they can't buy redemption for personal bondage nor by redemption for another person. Third, redemption from sin cannot be transferred from parents to children (verse 19). In the Old Testament, one's spiritual relationship with God came through the death of the perfect sacrificial lamb which was slain as part of Passover.

Christ's death on the cross provided redemption for all who will accept His offering of salvation from the bondage of sin. The Lamb of God, took on human flesh, and was crucified on that old cross to pay for our redemption. Because Christ has redeemed us from sin, we are not in command or independent control of our bodies. In the same way God owned the Hebrews due to His redemption of them from Egyptian bondage, He owns us as the result of our redemption from sin by Jesus taking our sin and being a sacrifice for our sin. This is what 1 Corinthians 6:20 tells about His Lordship, because we have been bought with a great price.

The price spoken about in verse 20, "For ye are bought with a price: therefore glorify God in your body, and in your spirit, which are God's," transfers ownership from ourselves with the burden of sin to our Savior. We deserved the punishment of death for our sins, but it was transferred to our Redeemer. Now as our Lord and Savior, He deserves all our praise and glory that we can give Him.

Moses was told by God that He was in control and would overcome the oppressive Egyptians. God told Moses that Israel was His chosen people. They were the smallest group of people at that time, according to (Deuteronomy 7:7), which says," for ye were the fewest of all people" and the next verse says," But because the Lord loved you, and because he would keep the oath which he had sworn unto your fathers, hath the Lord brought you out with a mighty hand, and redeemed you out of the house of bondmen, from the hand of Pharaoh King of Egypt.

When God chose to have a nation for Himself, He selected Abraham, who was a childless man. Their status as God's chosen people came from His sovereignty choosing to love them and to allow His blessings to flow over them. God's selection of Israel as His chosen people is also seen by His faithfulness, "the faithful God" (Deuteronomy 7:9).

Israel was to respond to God with responsibility on their part. They were to respond with obedience to His commandments out of love for the great God who had done so much for them but only a remnant loved and obeyed him.

According to 1 Peter 2:9,10 "We are a chosen generation, a royal priesthood, an holy nation." Just as God chose Israel to be His people, we enjoy this same status. Since Christ died on the cross, we enjoy the privilege of being priests who can go directly to the throne of God. We Christians have experienced regeneration and stand sanctified in His presence. In fact we can invite the Holy Ghost to live in our bodies which is the temple of the Holy Ghost.

Fanny Crosby wrote a hymn titled "Redeemed," praising God for her redemption: "Redeemed, how I love to proclaim it!/ Redeemed by the blood of the lamb;/ redeemed through His infinite mercy,/ His child, and forever, I am." I praise God also for His redemption of my soul and I intend to be His child forever.

One dictionary definition of redemption is, "to free from captivity by payment or ransom." That good old song "He set me free," is exactly what Jesus did for us when He gave His life on the cross for our sins. He paid the price which was His precious blood, to set us free from sin and death. The entire human race was separated from God when Adam and Eve disobeyed God by eating from the Tree of the Knowledge of Good and Evil.

Until Christ the Redeemer came, God provided a system of using the blood of bulls and goats to cover sins. But these sacrifices had to be used each day. And they had to be offered by a Levitical priest. Until the fullness of time God used this sacrificial system because He is sovereign and He has His own timetable.

God's holiness required a perfect sacrifice for sin and also one who could identify with humanity at the same time. That's why Jesus, took on human flesh, to become the sinless God-man. He knew man's weaknesses and temptations, yet never sinned (Hebrews 4:15).

Christ's mission as the Redeemer was told to James and John in (Mark 10:45), "For even the Son of man came not to be ministered unto, but to minister, and to give his life a ransom for many." In that same passage in Mark 10, James and John, approached Jesus with an unusual request: Could they sit on either side of Jesus in His Kingdom?

They asked for the two highest positions in His Kingdom. Jesus said, the greatness of God's leaders comes through servanthood. All of Christ's servanthood would not have fulfilled His mission without His death as the Redeemer. He gave His life as a ransom, so we could receive eternal life someday.

Christ served as the ransom, freeing humanity through becoming the exchange price. Through Christ's sacrificial death and subsequent resurrection, God released the sin which condemned and separated humanity. All that remains is for individuals, regardless of how many sins they have committed, to confess their sins and accept Jesus Christ as their Savior and Lord.

God's righteousness becomes our righteousness according to Romans 3:22-26. However, for the redemptive work of Christ to work in your life, you must believe. All we do is accept Jesus Christ as the saving Son of God and this opens the door for righteousness to come into our hearts.

We can never attain a righteousness acceptable to God, no matter how good we are or how hard we work. There is no way to earn righteousness or do away with our sinfulness through our human effort. We are only changed from sinners to Christians by the redemptive work of Jesus Christ, "Being justified freely by his grace through the redemption that is in Christ Jesus" (Romans 3:24).

God chooses to give his grace, which is the unmerited love and favor of God to man, which means declaring not guilty; acquittal in court of Heaven. When Christ died on the cross for us, it was a sacrificial death, which made justification available to all through faith in Christ. Then we receive God's righteousness in place of our sinful past.

We are able to experience total cleansing from sin, through the sacrificial death of our sinless Savior. We can experience cleansing from the sin of Adam and our personal sins. We experience eternal life here on earth with the promise of eternal life after death. Christ is our Redeemer.

There is no greater contrast in the world than the righteousness of God in comparison to the sinfulness of man.

The sinfulness of every person is a mark that we all have had on us. The question we all face is how we stand before a righteous God.

We can cheaply use the righteousness of God and the sinfulness of all men in Romans 3:21-26. However, "redemption" is provided by the righteousness of God, unto those that believe in Christ (verse 24). The word redemption literally means "ransom." This means the righteousness of God provides the payment for the debt of sinful man. The salvation of God provides redemption for sinful man, if man will believe and receive this free gift.

God's Saving act in Romans 6:23 states that, "For the wages of sin is death; but the gift of God is eternal life through Jesus Christ our Lord." Sin is the condition of man apart from God and the consequence is death. The fuller translation of "gift" could be "grace gift" and this meaning is, "favor given someone undeserving."

God cannot declare anybody righteous or take one of our sins away without us asking Him to, by faith in the blood of His Son. Man has used angels, voices from heaven, stars, and many other ways but none of these were sufficient for the full redemption of man. In the fullness of time, "God sent forth His Son, made of a woman, made unto the law."

It should be noticed that in Genesis 3:15 as well as in Galatians 4:4, it is the seed of the woman that is mentioned. This was a necessary fact it was not the seed of man so it could not only refer to the coming of the Messiah. God cannot die, but man can. It therefore became vital that the Son of God become human, the seed of, the Son of God and Mary.

Paul says, "the grace of God that bringeth salvation hath appeared to all men" (Titus 2:11), and salvation is for all. Verse 13, points us to the future. We are "looking for that blessed hope", until the fulfillment and fullness of pleasure will come with "the glorious appearing of the great God and our Savior Jesus Christ."

All Christians should be filled with the expectation of the blessed hope and the glorious appearing of Christ that all other matters are secondary. Christ is sure coming again for those who look for Him. The Bible says, "Who gave himself for us, that he might redeem us from all iniquity, and purify unto himself a peculiar people" (Deut 7:6). Which means Christians are now particular or unique or like Jesus "one of a kind."

The Christians only hope is in Christ, who gives us power to overcome the world. Belief that Jesus is the Christ is the core of Christianity. If we believe this we have life, light, and salvation, but if we don't believe this we have death, darkness and damnation. Spiritual life begins with the belief that Jesus Christ was the Son of God, sent by God the Father from heaven as a sacrifice for the sins of the world, whose blood cleanses us from sin. Everybody that believes this fact about Christ is born of God. Those who believe in Christ have life and those who do not believe in Christ remain in death.

The love for God the Father and Christ the Son amount to the same thing. To love one is to love the other and to reject one is to reject the other. Jesus said," He that hateth me hateth my Father also" (John 15:23). We also need to love and allow the Holy Spirit to guide us into all truth.

The Holy Ghost anointing which Jesus had is His service of redemption was prophesied 800 years before it was fulfilled, while Jesus was reading from Isaiah 61. Luke recorded the fulfillment of Isaiah's prophecy in Luke 3:16

The promise of the Holy Spirit filling believers in a baptismal measure is promised by Jesus in Luke 24:49, just before He ascended to Heaven. This promise was fulfilled in the fullness of time which was on the Day of Pentecost and recorded by Luke in Acts 2. Jesus was our example in water baptism and the baptizer in the Holy Spirit until our body is full and running over without measure into other souls. Then we have power to do extraordinary service for our Lord and Savior Jesus Christ.

The Holy Spirit in the Life of a person gives them power to fulfill His purpose. He comes and leads us to Jesus and makes alive in us the personality of Jesus because He comes to live in our bodies, which is the Temple of the Holy Ghost. The Holy Ghost leads into all truth but we must obey Him. The Spirit will not call us or lead us to anything that is contrary to the life of Jesus.

The Holy Spirit first anointed Jesus to "to preach good tidings unto the meek" and that makes it possible for the saints of God to hear the good tidings of God. One sentence of Jesus' fulfilling this is "Blessed are the meek: for they shall inherit the earth" (Matthew 5:5). The Meek are those who are humbled before the Lord. It does not necessarily mean they are weak persons; rather, they are those people who do the will of God and trust Him to care and to provide for them. The "meek" hears the good tidings and trusts God through the storms of life.

The anointed servant is also sent to "bind up the brokenhearted." In the Old Testament "Bind up" was used to speak of binding up a wound. Jesus always comforted those who were in distress and cared for them.

The anointing spoken of in Isaiah 61:1 was the ability to bind the "brokenhearted." The person was seen as a unity and thus the heart was used to describe the place of brokenness. If pain was experienced in one part of life, then other parts of life suffered as well. In Psalms 34:18 we read, "The Lord is nigh unto them that are of a broken heart." Also we find in Psalms other references such as, "Make me to hear joy and gladness; that the bones which thou hast broken may rejoice" (51:8); "He healeth the broken in heart, and bindeth up their wounds" (147:3).

The third thing the anointing gave Jesus power to do is "to proclaim liberty to the captives." The word "liberty" has the root meaning of "flowing, free run." Its parallel Arabic root focuses on "a stream flowing abundantly" and was used to describe rain and milk. In the New Testament it describes our love in relation to the law, and the brothers in the church. (Romans 8:21; 2 Corinthians, Galatians 5:13; James 1:25; 2:12)

"Captives" referred to those who were bound by the powers of an opposing force. In Isaiah 45: 13; 49:9; 51:14 it was used to describe the pitiful condition of the oppressed. Those who are "captives" are those who are held in bondage by an outside force.

"Prisoners" are those who are held because of their violation of laws of their land where they reside. The good news of the gospel promises that both the captives and the prisoners are set free in Christ.

The outside force, I believe is the power of demons that bind a person, Jesus can set them free; if it is the guilt of disobedience, Jesus can deliver. There is no prisoner that Jesus can't set free.

Job said "For I know my redeemer liveth, and that he shall stand at the latter day, upon the earth. We cannot know God unless He reveals Himself to us; human is not able to know Him as Savior unless His Spirit makes such revelation possible. We are able to know our redeemer lives because of Ephesians 1:18, which says, "The eyes of your understanding being enlightened; that ye may know what is the hope of his calling, and what is the riches of the glory of his inheritance in the saints."

The story of redemption was first hinted of in the Garden of Eden. (Genesis 3:15). In Chapter 12 God Blessed Abraham's seed. God called Abraham to become the founder of a nation having for its object the redemption of mankind.

God made a covenant with Abraham. The promise was that all of Abraham's descendants would be blessed; therefore that promise was to the Christian church, for the church is the true Israel and the true seed of Abraham. That blessing came true in Jesus Christ.

The covenant that Jesus spoke about was between God and man. Jesus spoke of His blood being the blood of the covenants. A covenant is a relationship between two people; when two people enter into a covenant, they enter into a relationship with each other. I'm glad that he was Son of

God and Son of man so his blood was able to honor this covenant, by God's son's precious blood.

In Matthew 26: 26-30 what Jesus was saying at the last supper was this: Because of my life, and above all because of my death, a new relationship is now possible between you and God. When Jesus said, "take eat; this is my body" (Verse 26) and the next verse said, "and he took the cup, and gave thanks and gave it them, saying, Drink ye all of it: For this is my blood of the New Testament, which is shed for many for the remission of sins." The promise was made, and the promises of God, like himself, are unchangeable and eternal.

Our salvation depends upon our reaction to what He has said. If we obey His message, our hope of redemption is realized. If we neglect His message, our doom is inevitable, according to Hebrews 2:3, "How shall we escape, if we neglect so great salvation." The failure to obey His word will result in tragic consequences.

God's word is binding on all because God's Son spoke these words in Hebrews 2:1, "Therefore we ought to give the more earnest heed to the things, which we have heard, lest at anytime we should let them slip." Since we know the Son has spoken, we must now pay much closer attention!

If the message of angels carried such great weight, the message from Christ is even weightier! The second verse says, "the word spoken by angels was binding, and every transgression, violation and disobedience received a just punishment." The message spoken by angels was binding. The fathers of Israel knew angels were present and were used in giving of the law in Acts 7:53. While God Himself gave the law to Moses, it is true that angels were involved in the events that accompanied the giving of the law.

Any violation of the law is met with just punishment. Any disobedience gets the appropriate penalty. One does not have the right to transgress the commandments of the Lord. The law of God and all the precepts of God are irrevocable. His law cannot be altered.

God's purpose for man is found in Hebrews 2:5-8. "For unto angels hath he not put in subjection the world to come, whereof we speak. But one on a certain place testified, saying, what is man, that thou are mindful of him? Or the son of man that thou visit's him?" God has used Christ and His followers to testify of salvation. He has used signs, wonders and many miracles. Though the manifestation of the gifts of the Holy Ghost which he has given according to His will, God has confirmed the gospel.

Angels have no moral responsibilities but God put man in charge of the works of His hands, and even says that there is nothing that is not subject to man. "Thou hast put all things in subjection under his feet. For in that he put all in subjection under him, he left nothing that is not put under him. But now we see not yet all things put under him" (Hebrews 2:8). In putting everything under him God left nothing that is not subject to him (man) yet at present we do not have everything subject to man because the Fall has marred and misdirected much of man's dominion. But it seems possible that if sin had not corrupted man's power, he could have, under God, extended the paradise of Eden over all the earth because this verse says, God put everything under man's feet.

At the present time everything is not subject to man. But that is man's fault. God said, "Because you listened to your wife and have eaten of the tree-cursed is the ground in sorrow shalt thou eat of it- thorns and thistles- sweat of thy face shalt thou eat bread" (Genesis 3:17-19). God's wisdom and understanding and fruit of righteousness is the tree of life. (Proverbs 11:30). Genesis 3:22,23 says," And the Lord God said, Behold, the man is become as one of us, to know good and evil; and now, lest he put forth his hand, and take also of the tree of life, and eat, and live forever: Therefore the Lord God sent him forth from the garden of Eden, to till the ground from whence he was taken."

God had to take man out of the garden because he sinned. The ground is cursed and many of the animals are no longer domesticated. Man can't enjoy the total dominion that God intended for him until all things are restored to God and salvation brings that about.

In the fullness of time God will create this new earth, to fulfill man's original destiny. The captain of Salvation (Hebrew 2:9), which means author or leader-one who originates something new will bring this to pass, in the fullness of time, according to this Scripture. "But we see Jesus, who was made a little lower than the angels for the suffering of death, crowned with glory and honor; that he by the grace of God should taste death for every man." The last phrase of next verse, "to make the captain of their salvation perfect through." The failure of man is here contrasted with the triumph of Jesus.

Christ's death was on behalf of all men. Through His death, He has made life possible for everyone. It was not nails that held him to the cross, it was love. Oh, what love! He did not go to the cross because man deserved for Him to go, but only because of His love and mercy for man. The Scripture says, Christ was made "perfect through suffering." What it means by "perfect" is the bringing to completion of the work Christ was sent to do. "For by one offering he hath perfected for ever them that are sanctified."

Christ is the only hope of the world. God's mercy and forgiveness of sins are extended to all through Jesus Christ. The Prophet Isaiah gave us a list of titles which shows His character and the mission of the Messiah. He said, "For unto us a child is born, unto us a son is given; and the government shall be upon his shoulder; and his name shall be called wonderful, counselor, the mighty God, the everlasting Father, the Prince of Peace" (Isaiah 9:6). In the fullness of time He was born where He was supposed to be born, His character and mission was full proof that He was the Messiah. He was called wonderful and He was wonderful in the whole bearing of His life. He was majestic in death and resurrection. He was counselor with His great wisdom and His ability to guide and direct the affairs of men. He would be both God and man no one else could make that claim because He had an earthly mother and Heavenly Father. "Mighty God" was a reference to His divine nature which was on His Father's side so He was Son of God and Son of man. Then, the Lord was called the "everlasting Father" because He is the Father of eternity, with His everlasting duration. He was also "The Prince of Peace." He was a peaceful prince. While He was walking on this earth, by His Word, His administration was to bring peace and encourage us to be peacemakers, when He said," blessed are the peacemakers; for they shall be called the children of God."

I'm glad that Jesus Christ is now our mediator, who sits beside His Father, to bring peace and reconciliation between God and man. The Lord Jesus Christ has received "a more excellent ministry," because "He is the mediator of a better covenant" according to Hebrews 8:6. In contrast with the ministries of the priests of old, the Lord Jesus Christ has received a ministry far superior to theirs because the above verse says "He had obtained a more excellent ministry." Also He is the mediator of a better covenant.

God in His wisdom and grace provided for the Church a new and better covenant. The other covenant, which was talked about, was the one God made with the children of Israel on Mount Sinai.

According to Hebrews 8:10-13, God could not enter into a new covenant with men to be "to them a God," and for them to be to Him "a people," while man was still fallen and sinful. So God provided a mediator of this new covenant, Jesus Christ, who would cleanse repentant man of his sin. Through Jesus, God secured all the good things of the covenant, to His grace and glory. In the covenant God became the mediator's master, and the mediator became the servant of God in a peculiar manner. It is peculiar because God, the mediator's master, became the Father; Christ, the mediator, became the Son; and we, the covenant people, became "heirs...and joint heirs with Christ" (Romans 8:17).

When the writer of Hebrews 7:25 says, "he is able to save," he is indicating that the priesthood of Christ combines intercession with the power to save. He has power to save and is now our High priest, to those who turn from sin and turn to God because" he is always living to plead on their behalf."

"Christ was once offered to bear the sins of many; and unto them that look for him shall he appear the second time without sin unto salvation" (Hebrews 9:28). Christ's death provides eternal redemption for all who believe. Christ was the perfect sacrifice and "by a greater and more perfect tabernacle, not made with hands, that is to say, not of this building." In Hebrews 9:11, the writers says the heavenly tabernacle out of which Christ ministers is a greater and more perfect tabernacle than "this building" which was fashioned by human hands or Solomon's hands. The whole majesty of God could only dwell in a temple not made by human hands. A testament is made by a living man; but while he lives, it is of no value. In order for it to be effectual, the testator must die. The writer of Hebrews in chapter 9:15-28 tells us we were redeemed by His blood and He is the mediator of the New Testament. The writer stresses the purpose of Christ's death. Without the shedding of His blood, the New Testament was meaningless. But when His precious blood was shed, the hope expressed in this covenant could be realized by any who would accept its promise by faith.

Upon his death, Christ, the testator, bequeathed His goods to His heirs. He was "appointed heir of all things" (Hebrews 1:2). In his death, He bequeathed "all things" unto His people, appointing them to be heirs of God and coheirs with Himself.

In the fullness of time God's voice will shake not only the earth, but also heaven. "Whose voice then shook the earth; but now he hath promised, saying, Yet once more I shake not the earth only, but also heaven" (Hebrews 12:26). The promise God made in this passage is that He will shake the earth again. The power of God is so great, when He spoke at Mount Sinai, the earth shook. "The whole mount quaked greatly" (Exodus 19:18).

The Holy Spirit gave the Apostle Peter unusual insight into the day when God will shake the heavens and the earth. "But beloved be not ignorant of this one thing, that one day is with the Lord as a thousand years, and a thousand years as one day. The Lord is not slack concerning his promise, as some men count slackness; but is longsuffering to us-ward, not willing that any should perish, but that all should come to repentance. But the day of the Lord will come as a thief in the night; in which that heavens shall pass away with a great noise and the elements shall melt with fervent heat. The earth also and the works that are therein shall be burned up. Seeing then that all these things shall be dissolved, what manner of persons ought ye to be in all holy conversation and godliness, looking for and hasting unto the coming of the day of God, wherein the heaven being on fire shall be dissolved, and the elements shall melt with fervent heat? Nevertheless we, according to his promise, look for new heavens and a new earth, wherein dwelleth righteousness" (2 Peter 3: 8-13).

In the fullness of time according to what the Holy Spirit inspired the Apostle Peter to write; all that has been created will be done away with. God told men in the Old Testament not to touch the mountain or they would die. They defied God and died. What will happen if they defy the grace of Christ Jesus because through His grace and mercy is the only way back to God. Peter says, "and if the righteous scarcely be saved, where shall the ungodly and the sinner appear?" (1 Peter 4:18).

"As it is written, There is none righteous, no not one,"(Romans 3:10), except God's son. God allowed no one but His Son to Redeem mankind. Moses was a great man and one of the best leaders on earth but God refused him when He offered to die to pay the ransom for the nation of Israel. God would not accept him because Moses was not a perfect sacrifice, which is God's requirement.

"But when the fullness of the time was come, God sent forth his Son, made of a woman, made under the law, to redeem them that were under the law, that we might receive the adoption of sons." As it is written there is none righteous, no, not one" (Romans 3:10). The reason that Apostle Paul made this statement is the Jews thought they had a better claim to the gospel than the Gentiles.

In the fullness of time Jesus became a human being, and being God himself, qualified Him to rescue all the people on earth and brought us into the Kingdom of his dear Son: "In whom we have redemption through his blood, even the forgiveness of sins: Who is the image of the invisible God the firstborn of every creature" (Colossians 1:14,15). I am so glad that God became flesh, in the person of Jesus Christ because humans can't become God.

God said, "I, even I, am the Lord; and beside me there is no savior" (Isaiah 43:11). The Lord is our Savior and Redeemer and according to Isaiah 42:8, all glory and praise is His when he said," I am the Lord; that is my name; and my glory will I not give to another, neither my praise to graven images." God said, in the next verse that He had foreknowledge of "new things" but "before they spring forth I tell you of them." God also says in Isaiah 49:26, "that I the Lord am they Savior and they Redeemer."

Yes, God's wonderful love promised to supply all our needs, which included a savior and redeemer when He said, "He that spared not his own Son, but delivered him up for us all, how shall he not with him also freely give us all things." God didn't even spare His own Son to give us all things according to Romans 8:32. This was the most precious gift God had to give to redeem us from sin.

When God created everything that was created, man was His greatest treasure because He could come down to earth and have fellowship with him. When the devil came down and told them many lies, they sold out to the devil. Now they needed someone to redeem themselves. God intervened, He promised to send the Redeemer, which was His precious Son.

Jesus said of Himself, "The Son of Man is come to seek and to save that which was lost" (Luke 19:10). God promised to send the Savior-Redeemer in His messianic prophecy (Genesis 3:15) because of sinful man. The Apostle Paul said, "But when the fullness of time was come, God sent forth His son, made of a woman, made under the law, to redeem them under the law, that we might receive the adoption of Sons" Galatians 4:4+5).

Jesus Christ is our Redeemer, the only mediator between God and men, because He died in our place; on the cross, by giving His life a ransom, for our sins. Because "all have sinned, and come short of the glory of God". When we believe in Christ as our Savior, we are "justified freely by His grace through the redemption that is in Christ Jesus".

To be redeemed by Christ is possible because God "set forth" (foreordained) Christ to be the all-sufficient sacrifice for our sins, so God forgives our sins for Christ's sake. We are given credit by God for the righteousness of Christ. This imparted righteousness of Christ, makes us righteous. As sinners, we are not acceptable to God, but having the righteousness of Christ, we become acceptable to Him.

To release Israel from Egyptian bondage, God sent plagues, but to redeem man He sent His Son to be the Redeemer. The dictionary says redeem means you can only redeem what you have once owned.

God is our creator but Adam's sin separated man from God. All the blessings of salvation come through our redemption by Son of God. If we have been rescued from Satan's control, we are "giving thanks unto the Father" and become patient, powerful, persistent, worshipful, people of God. We are headed for God's kingdom when we repent of our sin, trust in Christ and be the fruitful people God calls us to be.

The redeemed of the Lord should "give thanks" because "God is good" and delivers us from the enemy of our souls because "God is love." "O give thanks unto the Lord, for he is good: for his mercy endureth for ever. Let the redeemed of the Lord say so, whom he hath redeemed from the hand of the enemy" (Psalm 107:1-7). The Psalmist was thinking of Israel's redemption and journey from Egypt to Canaan.

Paul says, "In whom we have redemption through his blood, the forgiveness of sins, according to the riches of his grace; That in the dispensation of the fullness of times he might gather together in one all things in Christ, both which are in heaven, and which are on earth; even in him" (Eph:7+10). We can now be brought together through his blood, forgiveness of sins and look to Him to supply us with His wisdom and knowledge because all wisdom and knowledge comes from God. Christ is the head and we are the body.

Christ paid the full price to purchase us, but it is our decision to receive this gift, which is salvation, or reject the precious atoning blood of Jesus. Because of who Christ is," In whom we have redemption through his blood, even the forgiveness of sins; Who is the image of the invisible God, the firstborn of every creature; And he is before all things, and by him all things consist. And he is the head of the body, the church: who is the beginning, the firstborn from the dead; that in all things he might have the preeminence" (Colossians 1:14-18). Satan wants sinners to wait until tomorrow to receive this free gift of salvation.

TOMORROW

Tomorrow is just one more plan,
Satan use's to deceive everyone he can.
Yes he'll try his best to get you to delay.
And to put off the thing's you know you should do today.
By telling you wait till tomorrow you've got plenty of time,
Why waiting one more day won't be a crime.

But let me tell you about a man who listened to him,
And what happened to him in the end.

This man was a sinner but he went to church just about every morning service and night service too.
He felt since his family served the Lord this was the right thing to do,
So he would always go with them to encourage them in every way,
But every time he would feel God tugging at his heart he would never pray.

Sometimes he would feel God's calling so strong he'd grip the back of the pew,
And would keep saying in his heart not now Lord but someday I'll serve you.
Yes this would happen time and time again,
As Jesus beckoned to come in.

And it seemed like every message and every song touched him in some way,
But he kept saying not now Lord but I'll give you my heart one day.
And every time he would go to church he couldn't get away from that convicting feeling at all,
And would get up and go outside every time the preacher gave the altar call.

You see every time he kept rejecting Jesus never realizing what was happening to him,
Not knowing his heart was becoming hard and calloused with in.
When one night something was different and he couldn't understand what had changed.
The service's seemed so cold and he felt kind of strange.

You see for some reason it seemed the preacher's messages weren't as powerful as before.
Cause he didn't feel that tugging at his heart any more.

And it seemed like every time the choir would sing,
Night after night he couldn't feel anything.
And no longer preaching, testifying, or even a song,
Stirred his heart and he wondered what was wrong.

And as he sat and wondered what had happened Satan whispered in his ear,
Those were just emotion's you felt and by the way what are you doing here?
Why you could be out having so much fun with the other guy's,
And finally the man listened to Satan's lies.
He no longer wanted to go to church like he use to do,
He was too busy doing the thing's he wanted to.

Then while driving home on a rainy night in a terrible state,
As he was drunk and driving fast so he wouldn't get home too late.
He pressed on the gas hurrying to get home and he was almost there,
When a speeding car seemed to come out from nowhere.
And hit him head on and he was killed instantly,
And was found unprepared when he went out into eternity.
What a great loss and oh what a shame,
A man who's tomorrow never came!!!

Vanessa Taylor, 9-9-84

Heroes

As I sit here and think of life and all its many different stages;
I realize our heroes change right along with our ages.

When we were just tiny tots I guess our heroes were Santa Claus, Superman, and Captain Kangaroo;
Or maybe Mickey Mouse, Roy Rogers or Dale Evans, just to name a few.

But as we grew and time went on and we finally became a teen;
Our heroes may have changed to some singer or actor that caught our eye on the movie screen.

Or maybe it was someone we saw on the late night talk show;
Who caught our attention and became our hero.

But as we grow older it seems we begin to realize;
The ones who are the true heroes in our eyes.

An although the world may never even know their name;
In our eyes they're heroes just the same.

It may be that one who would get up all hours of the night;
To tip toe in each room making sure her little ones were tucked in tight.

Always sacrificing all the things she could have had;
For her family, yes, she's the girl who married dear ole Dad.

And in Dad's eyes somehow you knew there could never be another;
And you thanked your lucky stars for your life long friend, your hero, your mother.

Or maybe it was that special someone who worked hard with calloused hands
and by the sweat of his brow;
To make sure his wife and children had the things they needed somehow.

And at times it seems he worked so hard he'd never even take time to stop and rest;
Always striving to give his family the very, very best.

And always there to cheer you on days you were feeling kind of sad;
The man who married Mom, your life long friend, your hero, your Dad.

Your hero may be your husband or wife,
Or maybe the children God's given you to brighten your life.

Or maybe the men and women who fought and some who gave their lives for you and me; So we can live in America, the home of the brave and the land of the free.

And sometimes my mind goes to the future when all our troubles and trials are past;
And were all standing n the presence of our Lord and Savior at last.

And as we lift up our eyes to behold Jesus face to face;
The greatest Hero of every man, woman, boy and girl of every color and race.

As we look around to the ones who helped us to make it through;
We can thank our Lord personally for being a friend that sticketh closer than a brother a friend we found to be true.

Who never left us our whole lives journey but was there where ever we would go;
Our Counselor, Savior, Redeemer, The Beginning, and The End, Life Long Friend, our Hero!!!

Vanessa Taylor, 4-25-91

We all know that the Father, Christ the Son, and the Holy Spirit, created everything that was created because God said, "let us make man in our own image" (Genesis 1:26). We all know Christ had a part in creating man. "Therefore if any man be in Christ, he is a new creature; old things are passed away; behold, all things become new" (2 Cor. 5:17).

I'm glad that I am now an "ambassador for Christ" and reconciled to God. The apostle Paul said, "For he hath made him to be sin for us, who knew no sin; that we might be made the righteousness of God in him."

Paul also says," For it pleased the Father that in him should all fullness dwell," he goes on to say, He made "peace through the blood of his cross to reconcile all things unto himself, in earth and things in heaven" (Col. 1:19+20) he will complete in the millennium.

Paul also said Christ is the fullness--the fulfillment, the completion--and the Father gave Christ the power to be our Judge, our Savior, our Redeemer, that the fullness of divinity should reside in Christ. Through Christ God reconciled all things unto Himself. Through Faith in Christ's finished work we can have peace with God and man.

According to Ephesians 1:7 we have redemption through the blood of Christ and forgiveness of Sins, "according to the riches of his grace." Then verse 10 says, "That in the dispensation of the fullness of times he might gather together in one all things in Christ, both which are in heaven and which are on earth; even in him." God says, that Christ is the head of all. Times past, time present and time to come will all converge in Jesus Christ.

God is pleased to redeem us, "that in the dispensation of times (in the fullness of time) he might gather together in one (God's purpose) all things in Christ, both which are in heaven and which are on earth, even in him" (Ephesians 1:9+10). This is how Christ is made head of all things. This will be fulfilled in the millennium when all enemies will be defeated and Christ is head over all.

Since Christ is head of all things, we must realize and acknowledge He died for our sins, because "all have sinned, and come short of the glory of God" (Romans 3:23). Yes, we all have come short of Heaven because of sin. We must realize and acknowledge, "the wages of sin is death" (Romans 6:23). All men die physically, but all men do not die spiritually. Everyone can be born again through Jesus Christ and be saved from the penalty of sin, which is an eternal Hell, a place of "fire and brimstone; which is the second death" (Revelation 21:8).

We must realize and acknowledge: "Christ died for our sins" (1 Corinthians 15:8). Jesus Christ paid the total price on the cross for our sins. We must realize and acknowledge: the gift of God is eternal life through Jesus Christ our Lord" (Romans 6:23).

God offers us freely His gift of eternal life. This gift is for everyone by believing in a risen Christ who arose on the third day and is alive forever more. We must realize and acknowledge that "whosoever shall call upon the name of the Lord shall be saved (Romans 10:13).

In Chapter 3 of Ecclesiastes Solomon says, our fleshly bodies dye, but the spirit of man can live forever. He preached on his experience and reflections but did not follow his own wisdom. Proof of Solomon's backsliding is found in Eccl. 2:10 where he fulfilled every lust and whatever his eyes desired to look at.

God gave Solomon a lot of wisdom because this is what he desired of God. Wisdom and knowledge only comes from God. In Eccl. 3:1, he said, "To every thing there is a season, and a time to every purpose under the heaven:" then goes on to give us twenty-eight seasons of life. In the fullness of time all will be fulfilled, which includes, "a time to be born, and a time to die."

While we live on this earth, God loves us so much that He allows us to choose which one we will serve. Our choice is God or Satan. There are two places we can choose to spend eternity. Our choice can be Heaven, where Jesus has gone to prepare for the Christians, or we can choose Hell, which was prepared for the devil and his angels. The choice for eternity is very clear, it is Heaven or Hell. God will not make us go to Heaven or Hell, but if we choose the devil to be our master, Hell will be our eternal abode, but we can choose Jesus Christ as our Lord and Savior and live with Him forever.

PART IV

Christ the Healer

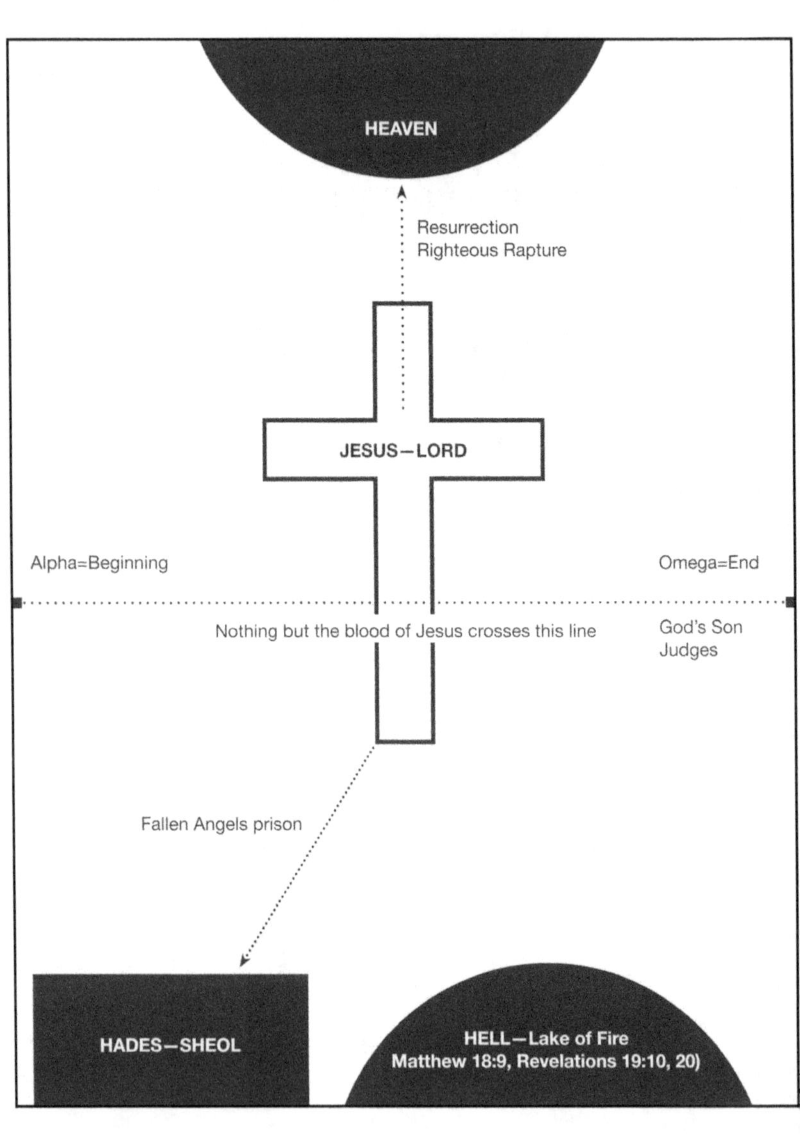
HEAVEN
Resurrection
Righteous Rapture
JESUS—LORD
Alpha=Beginning
Omega=End
Nothing but the blood of Jesus crosses this line
God's Son
Judges
Fallen Angels prison
HADES—SHEOL
HELL—Lake of Fire
Matthew 18:9, Revelations 19:10, 20)

JOHN GIVES THIS REASON for recording the life of our miracle-working Lord; "But these are written, that ye might believe that Jesus is the Christ, the Son of God; and that believing ye might have life through his name" (John 20:31). There were thirty- six miracles which were done by Christ prior to His crucifixion. Some dealt with one person; others, with multitudes.

Christ healed many people that were not recorded. Christ healed men and women, boys and girls, Jews and non-Jews, people present and people absent. Some He touched, to others He merely spoke. Three dead people were revived. The first was the twelve-year-old daughter of Jairus. Word came to Jairus that the child was already dead. Nevertheless, Jesus went to the home and at his word, "her spirit came again, and she arose" (Luke 8:55).

The second case concerns the only son of a widow of the city of Nain. He had been dead several hours. Jesus came to him and said, "Young man, I say unto thee, arise" (Luke 7:4).

Jesus came into the world to be a Savior, however, while doing His ministry of redemption, He did many wonderful miracles. The working of miracles was an important part of the Lord's work, but by no means the principle part.

I will list eighteen recorded healings before the cross as follows:

1. The sick son of a nobleman (John 4:46-54)
2. Peter's mother-in-law with a fever (Matthew 8:14-17)
3. Leper of Capernaum (Mark 1:40-45)
4. Paralytic of Capernaum (Matthew 9:1-8)
5. Impotent man of Jerusalem (John 5:1-9)
6. Man with a withered hand (Matthew 12:10-13)
7. Centurion's servant, palsy (Matthew 8:5-8)
8. Woman with issue of blood (Matthew 9: 20-22)
9. Blind men of Capernaum (Matthew 9:27-31)
10. Syrophoenician's daughter (Matthew 15:21-28)
11. Deaf-mute of Galilee (Mark 7: 31-37)
12. Blind man of Bethsaida (Mark 8:22-26)
13. Ten lepers of Samaria (Luke 17:11-19)
14. Blind man at Jerusalem (John 9:1-7)
15. Woman with infirmity (Luke 13:11-17)
16. Man with dropsy (Luke 14:1-6)
17. Blind Bartimaeus of Jericho (Mark 10:46-52)
18. Servants ear replaced (Luke 22: 50,51)

Jesus did these miracles and others will be gone into more in detail later on in this book. Through these miraculous manifestations many believe that Jesus was the Christ and thereby received everlasting life.

This is the justification of seeking God for healings. Consider, "And now, Lord, behold their threatenings; and grant unto thy servants, that with all boldness they may speak thy word. By stretching forth thine hand to heal; and that signs and wonders may be done by the name of thy holy child Jesus" (Acts 4:29,30).

In the early church miracles did not cease when Jesus ascended to heaven. He said, "Ye shall receive power, after that the Holy Ghost is come upon you" (Acts 1:8). He also said, "Verily, verily, I say unto you, He that believeth on me, the works that I do shall he do also; and greater works than these shall he do; because I go unto my father" (John 14:12).

Today His promise that we would do "greater works" is being fulfilled. Any Christian can be involved in the Spirit's work. Miracles are still happening according to Psalm 103:2, which states, "Bless the Lord, O my soul, and forget not all his benefits." Then a list is made: He forgives iniquities, heals diseases, redeems from destruction, crowns with loving-kindness, and satisfies hunger.

Signs and wonders show that God is in the now, working miracles and is in immediate connection with the human family and that His presence is loving and healing. God depends on human hands and committed hearts to be used as instruments in His hands to be used for His glory, which provide revelation and edification.

His miracles under girded His ministry and emphasized it. Jesus did not perform miracles for His own benefit or convenience. He always blessed other people but did not do it as a profession.

If we have the gift of healing, it should be a calling and not a career. If we follow in the way of Christ, then we will spend our lives seeking the good of our fellowman. In Luke 19:10 He said," For the Son of man is come to seek and to save that which was lost." The working of miracles was an important part of the Lord's work but by no means the principle part.

Jesus grew up with his parents in Nazareth and was subject to them Luke 2:51. He was obedient to His parent's wishes when he was only twelve years old. He still needed that parental nurture which His godly parents would continue to give Him the next several years. Mary, after finding Jesus talking with the doctors of the law in Jerusalem, was more puzzled over her son.

Although His true nature and His actual mission must yet have been only dimly apparent to her, she knew that He was Messiah, and she must have wondered how he was going to grow up and fulfill His destiny.

Jesus, according to Luke 1:52, achieved a fourfold growth into maturity. He matured physically intellectually, socially, and spiritually according to this verse. The total effect is that the child Jesus grew into His adulthood under the approval of men and God. At the time of childhood men could only see a godly child growing up with spiritual values. Jesus increased... in favor with God. He always pleased His heavenly Father. He was a perfect child and a perfect man, God's perfect sacrifice for our sins.

Jesus did miracles as the Son of God. He declared in the synagogue at Nazareth, quoting Isaiah 61:1,2- "The Spirit of the Lord is upon me, because he hath anointed me to preach the gospel to the poor; he hath sent me to heal the brokenhearted, to preach deliverance to the captives, and recovering of sight, to the blind, to set at liberty them that are bruised, to preach the acceptable year of the Lord" (Luke 4:18,19).

Although Jesus grew up with His family in Nazareth, Jesus moved to Capernaum when He began His public ministry. Matthew 4:13 says, "and leaving Nazareth, he came and dwelt in Capernaum." The people of Nazareth rejected Christ and His ministry. Capernaum was a much larger city with many more people to be reached with the gospel.

In Mark 1:23 an unclean spirit was in a man, a demon-possessed man in the synagogue where Jesus came to worship. The demon witnessed immediately to Jesus' divinity: "I know thee who thou art, the Holy one of God. And Jesus rebuked him, saying, Hold thy peace, and come out of him" (Verses 24-25). The fact that Jesus told the demon be quiet, shows the total authority of Jesus and makes it clear that Satan and his demonic forces operate only with permission and with limited authority.

During His Galilean ministry, He resided at the home of Simon (Verse 29). In verse 30, Jesus discovered that Peter's mother-in-law lay sick of a fever. He simply took her by the hand and lifted her up; and in verse 31 she immediately prepared both the master and her household something to eat. That evening all the city came and brought unto him all that were diseased, and them that were possessed with devils. Jesus healed many that was sick of many diseases and cast out many devils (Verse 34). He refused to allow the devils to speak, perhaps He knew that talk of His messiahship would cause Him more persecution and cut short His Galilean ministry. The demons confession of His Divinity, might have created suspicion or lead even to allegations, like those by the Pharisees later. Jesus got out of bed way before daylight (verse 35), the disciples were following Him (Verse 36) and couldn't understand His need for prayer, nor could they understand the main purpose of his ministry. The disciples were just beginning their training period; hence, they disturbed His prayer time to tell all men sought his healing. In verse 38 tells us He was praying. His central purpose was proclaiming the gospel. In verse 39 of Mark, Jesus refused to be sidetracked from His mission to preach. In the first chapter of Mark we see compassionate Christ who wears Himself out and ministers to all who suffer from physical, psychological, or spiritual maladies. We also see him cleansing a Leper that makes foolish statements when he said to Jesus, "If you want to, you can make me clean" (verse 40-45). These words were followed by the Masters healing touch. "I want to" he said, touching the man and making him clean. We see a compassionate Christ who did not want anybody to suffer and we also see a responsible Christ who insists that He not be sidetracked from His central saving mission- a Christ who keeps a proper balance among the priorities of His ministry, even if He was misunderstood by His chosen followers.

According to Matthew 4:23, Jesus was the Teacher, Preacher, and Healer. To the crowds Jesus preached the Kingdom of God, but to the disciples, He taught or declared the mysteries of God, which is a secret previously hidden but now made clear to all who will accept the truth. Unlike the disciples of the Pharisees who followed a rabbi, the disciples of Christ were called to a lifestyle with totally new requirements. They were required by Christ to live what He taught. He taught them that His Father's law had been misinterpreted, mishandled, and misunderstood (Mark 3:2-5; Luke 5:29-32; 7:36-50) and that He had come to fulfill the law.

In teaching about life within the kingdom, He declared a new kind of righteousness, exceeding that of the scribes and Pharisees (Matthew 5:20). He set love as the standard which the life of God was to flow through the believers unto the world (Matthew 22:35-40). Men, like trees, were also to be known by their fruit (Matthew 7:16-20).

Jesus acted always for man, never against him. The kingdom means blessings and not cursing, mercy and not wrath. All the multitude who gathered (regardless of their motive) were fed. All the sick were healed. None was turned away, because they were found "unworthy," and no one qualified because he was "good" or because of the "color" of their skin. No matter if they had weak or strong faith, God's wonderful compassion was there for all who reached out to Jesus for their need.

After spending a little time in Judea, Jesus returned to Galilee. Jesus took the most direct route through Samaria-despite the common custom of the Jews to go around that mixed Jewish and non-Jewish people. His meeting with the woman at Jacob's well resulted not only in her conversion but that of her entire village. This new acceptance of the Gospel made possible a fuller release of His power, a greater ministry of healing, deliverance, preaching and teaching of the Gospel. In the fullness of time, after waiting on the Holy Spirits anointing, Jesus turned the water into wine (John

4:46). In this same verse of scripture we find a nobleman from Capernaum came to Cana to get Jesus to return with him and heal his dying son. He had heard of Jesus' power to work miracles but did not know anything else of His nature. The nobleman's son was "at the point of death" and the father had no idea that to Jesus death itself was no problem. Jesus told the father in (John 4:50) "Go home, your son lives."

The nobleman's faith was weak because of his limited contact with the Word-Jesus Christ the word in person but the Word told us how to have faith in (Roman 10:17). "So then faith cometh by hearing and hearing by the word of God."

Confirmation of the nobleman's son being healed caused him to believe (John 4:53) because he discovered that at the moment when Jesus declared "Your son lives" the fever left and his whole house believed. Turning the water into wine and healing the nobleman's son was Jesus' way of meeting earthly needs. God can meet our needs, but it seems God will only do this when we believe that He can. It seems that God's miracle- working power can't work without faith and if He is willing and we must believe that He can do it. Jesus did not come into the world to be a healer only but the greatest miracle is being a Savior. Jesus healed and saved many in His ministry. In Luke 19:10 He said, "For the Son of man is come to seek and to save that which was lost." The working of miracles was an important part of the Lord's work, but wasn't the principal part.

Jesus was a very compassionate Savior (John 5:5-9). When Jesus saw the man, Jesus asked him if he wished to be made whole, (verse 6). In verse 8, Jesus commanded the man to, "Rise, take up thy bed, and walk." The next verse (Verse 9), the man was instantly healed. The man arose, rolled up his bed, and walked as the Lord told him to do.

Matthew 7:29 says," he taught them as one having authority, and not as the scribes." Jesus had given His famous sermon on the Mount near Capernaum.

At the conclusion of His sermon on the mount, He started back toward Simon Peter's house in Capernaum. Great multitudes followed Him down the mountain (8:1). When a leper broke through the multitude and appealed to Jesus for healing, Jesus "put forth his hand and touched him." The result was that "immediately his leprosy was cleansed." Because He did not want to be known primarily as a healer, Jesus told the man to tell no one, but to follow the Mosaic ritual of thanksgiving. Jesus went from the mountain into Capernaum, teaching and healing as He went. Before He could reach Peter's house (Matthew 8:14), the encounter with the Roman Centurion occurred.

Capernaum was a principle city of Galilee, so troops were stationed there. Upon entering Capernaum Jesus was met by a Roman Centurion (Matthew 8:5). He was an officer of authority and command. Although his name was not given, there was another Roman Centurion whose name we do know: Cornelius, who was filled with the Holy Spirit under the ministry of Peter (Acts 10:1). This indicates that a number of Roman soldiers were attracted to the gospel of Jesus Christ (Matthew 8:6) says, he addressed Jesus respectfully as "Lord God," which shows he recognized him as a person of great authority.

The centurion's request concerned his servant who was a paralytic, so infirm that he was confined to his bed, "my servant liveth at home sick of the palsy" (Matthew 8:6). In verse 7, Jesus offered to come with the centurion and heal his servant. The centurion said, he did not feel worthy for Christ to come into his house (Matthew 5:8). Although he may not have recognized Jesus as the Son of God, he recognized Him as a spiritual leader. He thought of himself to be a rough and rude man of the world. This is why he felt unworthy for the Lord to come under his roof. The centurion was able by a word to send soldiers against an enemy or gain victory against the enemy. He recognized that Jesus could send the spiritual agents to overcome sickness and disease of sin and evil. The centurion knew that just as he had power and authority in the military world, so Jesus had power and authority in the spiritual world. The centurion could give orders and have them obeyed even when he was not physically present, so could Jesus give orders from afar and have them obeyed (Matthew 8:9). Jesus commended the centurions faith in (Matthew 8:13), and told him his servant would be healed.

It is the exercise of faith that opens God's door of mercy and blessing which He has for us, by believing in Him and His word. The centurion could have desired his servants healing and yet have done nothing about it. And the servant would have died. It is by the exercise of what faith we have that more faith is given to us, and when we believe, all things are possible unto us "as thou has believed, so be it done unto thee" (Matthew 8:13). The believing Jesus spoke of here is a believing from the heart: "for with the heart man believeth unto righteousness" (Romans 10:10) a person is saved by faith, healed by faith, and without faith it is impossible to please God (Hebrews 11:1). Since I am a graduate of D.L. Moody Bible Institute, I'd like to quote Dwight L. Moody's three kinds of faith in Jesus Christ: which is struggling faith, it is like a man in deep water; clinging faith, which is like a man hanging to the side of a boat; and resting faith, which finds a man safely within the boat, and able moreover to reach out with a hand to help someone else.

Jesus showed he had authority over death (Luke 7:13-15). As Jesus and His disciples seen this funeral procession, Jesus was moved with compassion when He saw this mother, which was in front of the casket of her dead son. Jesus said to her, "weep not." This woman was a widow and this was here only son. She who had already lost her husband, now had lost her son. In those days there was no social assistance programs for persons without any providers. In that day and time the men were providers and protectors of the women and family.

It was the Jewish custom of that day if anyone touch the dead, or touched the coffin where they lay were unclean. Yet, Jesus laid His hand on the coffin and said, "Young man, I say unto thee, Arise" (Luke 7:14). I have called, where the boy lay dead, a coffin but it was a bier, which was the flat rigid slab upon which the dead was carried to the grave. A bier might be either a wooden board or a thin slab of stone. Jesus spoke to the young man and told him to arise, However in Luke 7:15, he not only sat up, but also began to speak. This act of restoring life to the dead, is not the same as will happen at the resurrection in the last days.

In the resurrection, men will be raised from the dead unto eternal life; but in this case the boy was simply restored to his natural life. This is the meaning of the words "he delivered him to his mother." When Jesus raised the dead to life again, He always spoke directly to the dead person. To the young man, He said, "Young man I say unto thee, Arise" (Luke 7:14). To Jarus's daughter He said, "Maid arise" (Luke 8:54). He said, to Lazarus, "Lazarus, come forth" (John 11:43). In (Luke 7:22), Jesus sent word to John the Baptist, "that the dead are raised," which probably means more than the three we read about in the New Testament took place because He is as much the Lord of the dead as He is lord of the living.

The Spirit came upon the Prophets to do certain miracles but God gave the Spirit without measure to Christ and the Spirit remained on Him. The Prophets had the mosaic portion in Numbers 11:17-25, Elijah had a portion in Kings 2:9, Elisha received a double portion which proves there are different measures of the Holy Spirit and power. John the Baptist was given a portion of the Spirit of Elijah Luke 1:15-17, however God gave the Holy Spirit without measure to Christ and the Spirit remained on Him. God wants us to be filled in the same measure and "to know the love of Christ, that we might be filled with all the fullness of God" (Ephesians 3:19).

Christ was the Messiah but they only thought of Him as "a great prophet" (Luke 7:16). The people were spiritually blind, because they did not see him as the Messiah. The Prophet Elijah had raised the son of the widow of Zarephath (1 Kings 17: 17-24), and Elisha had restored the son of the Shunamite woman to life again (2 Kings 4:32-37).

The Old Testament prophets had done great works, so it was assumed that Jesus was another in the prophetic line. Jesus proved to be the lord of life and of death by performing these two miracles on successive days. He healed the Centurion's servant by speaking from afar. Now He proved Himself to be Lord of Death and the grave. Time, space, sickness, and death were all obedient to Him, for He was and is now the divine Lord of all things. In the fullness of time, the Lord will raise our love ones from the grave!

The disciples rebuked those that brought children to Jesus. But Jesus said, "Let the children come to me" (Matthew 19:14). The disciples also wanted Jesus to get rid of the Syrophoenician woman because she was a Gentile and belonged to the old Canaanite stock and the Canaanites were the ancestral enemies of the Jews. In contrast to the selfish attitude of the disciples, Jesus was moved with compassion toward this woman. He told her in (Matthew 15:24), at this time He was sent "but unto the lost sheep of the house of Israel," but the commission to reach the whole world would come latter. This woman was very persistent. She came and knelt before Him and said: "Lord help me," (Matthew 15:25). He answered and said, "It is not meet to take the children's bread, and cast it to dogs." In Matthew 15:27, she said, "Truth, Lord; yet the dogs eat of the crumbs which fall from their masters table." This woman's faith was so strong, she believed He would help her and make her daughter whole. He said in verse 28, "O woman, great is thy faith." Jesus told her, you may go; the demon has left your daughter." All she had to do was to go home and find her daughter healed because Jesus said to the woman, "Be it unto thee even as thou wilt."

After Jesus arrived at the Sea of Galilee, He went up into a mountain and sat down. Great multitudes came to Him bringing all that were physically and mentally sick and he healed them. Matthew 15:30 says, Great Multitudes came and having with them the sick which included; "those that were lame, blind, dumb, maimed and many others and cast them down at Jesus' feet; and he healed them." No wonder the psalmist says; "Great is the lord, and greatly to be praised; and his greatness is unsearchable" (Psalm 145:3). A miracle always calls attention to the Lord and glorifies His great name. Matthew says, "they glorified the God of Israel."

Mark 9:18 says," and wheresoever he taketh him, he teareth him; and he foameth, and gnasheth with his teeth, and pineth away; and I spake to thy disciples that they should cast him out; and they could not." The father told of his son's reaction to the demon that possessed him. The boy was thrown into severe convulsions; he foamed at the mouth and was made to grind his teeth and became very rigid in body. The demon had complete control of the boy. The father told Jesus that he brought his son to the disciples and they could not heal him. Jesus asked his father, "How long is it ago since this came unto him? And he said, of a child," (Mark 9:21). The father told Jesus his son has been afflicted of this evil spirit from childhood. The next verse, he says to Jesus: "If you can do anything, take pity on us and help us." Jesus said, "what do you mean, If you can? Everything is possible for him who believes." The father said, "I do believe." Then he prayed, "Help me overcome my unbelief!" the real problem was this unbelief when the devil was cast out the boy looked like a dead person, in fact many of the people said, "He's dead." But Jesus took him by the hand and lifted him to his feet, and he stood up healed.

This lets us know we can: "Resist the devil and he will flee from you" (James 4:7). Even though the devil may cast you to the ground or you may fall many times, you can always rise up in the name of Jesus because you always can have victory in His precious name. When Satan is reminded of the blood of Jesus, he trembles. He knows that Jesus is the way and that he cannot stop those who find Jesus. He knows that Jesus is the truth and the truth shows who he is. The devil knows that Jesus is the life and everyone who has Jesus is spared the destruction and death of the devil. To answer the question, "Why could not we cast him out?" Matthew 17:20 says, "Because you have so little faith, if you have faith as small as a mustard seed, you can say to this mountain, move from here to there and it will move. Nothing will be impossible for you." In Luke 17:5,6, Jesus tells His disciples: "If you have faith as small as a mustard seed, you can say to this mulberry tree, "be uprooted and planted in the sea," and it will obey you." If we trust Him, He will never let us down and we know that, all things are possible to him that believeth" (Mark 9:23).

Jesus' reason for healing the man born blind was that God might be glorified. That was the objective behind everything He did was to glorify God. This should be the motivation behind the efforts of all believers. This blind man was not suffering as the result of his sin or his parent's sin. In the mind of the Jews this was possible because they believed that illness always came because of sin in the victim's life. We suffer because we are a fallen race, and we are a fallen race because we and our forbears have been disobedient to the will of God. But it is not true that every sickness can be traced back to somebody's particular sin. Jesus made it plain in John 9:3, that this man's blindness was not the result of any specific sin. This was an opportunity for God to show man His power and mercy in operation. When the blind man obeyed Christ after "He spit on the ground, made some mud with the saliva, and put it on the man's eyes," and said, "Go wash in the pool of Siloam," and John 9:7 says, "He washed, and came seeing." Obedience played a very important part in the blind man being delivered of his blindness. "I was blind but now I see" is the testimony every believer can give. Jesus passed through Jericho, which was about fifteen miles from Jerusalem. He was surrounded by many people. Jesus always had a crowd around Him because He taught while He walked. This was one of the commonest ways of teaching at this time. At this time the law required every male Jew over twelve years of age who lived within fifteen miles of Jerusalem must attend the Passover. Those who could not go lined the streets of the towns to encourage them to go on this occasion, the crowd must have swelled to capacity because of the young Galilean, who was a hero to many, was in the crowd.

As Jesus was passing through Jericho for the last time, a blind man named Bartimaeus heard the crowd coming, and asked who was attracting this attention. When they told him it was Jesus, he cried out to Jesus for help: "He began to cry out, and say, Jesus, thou son of David, have mercy on me" (Mark 10:47). He must have known the Hebrew equivalent of His name is Joshua, which means "Jehovah the Savior" or "Jehovah will save."

The people with Jesus were trying to make the blind man be quiet but Bartimaeus was determined to get out of his world of darkness and into the light. To them, Bartimaeus was worth nothing, but to Christ he was an eternal priceless soul. Bartimaeus had to overcome every obstacle that stood in his way. Jesus heard his cry and Mark 10:49 says," Jesus stood still, and commanded him to be called. And they call the blind man, saying unto him, "Be of good comfort, rise; he calleth thee" (Mark 10:49).When we pray to Jesus, we can rest assured, He will stand still and hear our cry also. Jesus tells us in Mark 11:24,"What things sover ye desire, when ye pray, believe that ye receive them, and ye shall have them." Blind Bartimaeus believed and received his sight. We can believe and receive because He is no respecter of persons. Jesus said to him, "Go thy way; thy faith hath made thee whole. And immediately he received his sight, and followed Jesus in the way" (Mark 10:52). Jesus declared him healed." Go", He said, "Your faith has healed you." The exercise of faith still brings deliverance. We receive this healing by faith and miss it by our lack of faith. According to Mark 6:5, when Jesus was in Nazareth He could not do any miracles there, and only healed a few sick people, because of their lack of faith. Jesus is looking for people who will follow Him after their deliverance, like Bartimaeus. Peter walking on the water began to sink but said," Lord save me," "Lord I want to see" and Jesus caused both to be able to follow Him.

On the Journey to Jerusalem, ten men that were lepers were a long way from Jesus but according to Luke 17:13, "They lifted up their voices, and said, Master, have mercy on us." This was a cry as desperate as Bartimaeus'. All of humanity has to cry as these men did for deliverance from sin. We all need the cleansing power of Christ to make us whole and set us in right relationship again with God and with our fellowmen. We were saved by crying out to God for His mercy. Jesus required the ten lepers to go and be examined by the priest and to be pronounced clean. This required faith on their part of Christ's power of healing them. Some people Christ healed instantly, but others were required to do something, like the ten lepers. The main thing is do what the Master asks. We have no right to ask the Lord whatsoever we will unless we are doing whatsoever He commands, because He will always do His part when we do our part. As the lepers were on their way, they were cleansed. Jesus could just as well have performed the miracle when they were in His presence, but he chose to test their faith. The miracle of healing took place as they obeyed Him. When one of the lepers realized that he was healed, he came back to Jesus, praising God in a loud voice. Now, instead of decaying, raw flesh, he had clean, new skin. He could now go anywhere with anybody, and not have to say," unclean." Ten lepers were healed, but only one thanked him after being healed. The others went on their way; he returned and threw himself at Jesus' feet and thanked him.

Lazarus, Mary, and Martha were personal friends of Jesus and Jesus loved them very much. They lived in Bethany which is located about two miles southeast of Jerusalem. It seems that Jesus stayed in their home in Bethany many days. One day Mary showed her affection for Jesus by anointing Him with costly perfume. Martha loved him so much that she worked like a slave in the Kitchen preparing Him meals.

When Lazarus became seriously ill, the two sisters sent word to Jesus, but when Jesus heard the news of his illness, He did not go directly to them as they thought. "When he heard this, Jesus said, This sickness is not unto death, but for the glory of God, that the Son of God might be glorified there by" (John 11:4). The lesson for us believers is that if a man chooses to serve God, then that man's day will not end before God desires it to end.

Jesus told the disciples that Lazarus is asleep and that He is going to wake him up. They did not understand that Jesus meant Lazarus was dead. They thought if he was asleep, then, he would soon be better. When Jesus arrived at the house where His friends lived, He found out that Lazarus had been in the tomb for four days. Many people were at the house to comfort them in the loss of Lazarus, their brother because visits of sympathy to the sorrowing friends and relations on one who had died were an essential part of Jewish religion. In John 11:39, "Jesus said, Take ye away the stone." Martha, the sister of him that was dead, saith unto him, Lord, by this time he stinketh; for he hath been dead four days." Martha objected saying that Lazarus had been dead for four days and that by this time there would be a bad odor. But Jesus told her that she was about to see the glory of God.

He called upon men to do what men could do. Men couldn't raise Lazareth from the dead, but they could roll away the stone. Men also were used by Christ to move the grave clothes. When this was done, no one could deny he was dead, because they smelled the stench of death. When Lazareth was raised from the dead, nobody could deny that this was a notable miracle.

The dead man in John 11: 44, came forth while still wrapped in his grave clothes. This was a great miracle to raise a man from the dead who had been in the grave for 4 days. Isaiah has been in the grave several thousand years yet he said "our dead men shall live, together with my dead body shall they arise" (Isaiah 26:19).

The Rapture

Soon Jesus will split the eastern sky,
And millions will be gone in a twinkle of an eye.
For us that will be a glorious day,
But how terrible for those who will be left here to stay.

I imagine the newsman will come on T.V.,
With the most shocking news they'll ever be.
As he tries to explain on that day,
How millions have suddenly vanished away.

He'll say something drastic has happened that can't be denied,
As millions are missing, even graves have burst open wide.
And hospitals have reported the strangest thing,
They say all the babies are gone from the newborn wings.

And we have reports coming in,
That all are gone who claim to be born again.
And there have been so many tragedies,
Because some drivers of cars have disappeared so suddenly.

Yes tragedies have been happening everywhere,
Some have taken place in the air.

As pilots of planes have disappeared too,
I've never had to report so much bad news.

Yes many are weeping because the ones they loved so dear,
Have somehow mysteriously disappeared.
And there are some crying out,
Who claim to know what this disappearance is all about.

So let's point the cameras to some of the people who have come here today,
And lets listen to what they have to say.
As the cameras point to a man with tears running down his face,
He says everyone listen very closely because I believe I know what's just took place.

You see I went to church with my wife now and then,
And the people there claimed that Jesus would come again.
And I believe that's what's happened you see,
And that explains why He didn't take me.

But we chose to reject God's only Son,
And now we're suffering for what we've
done.
Well the cameraman say's I'm running out of time,
So I'll close tonight's news with a conclusion of mine, Jesus has come and we've been left behind!!!

Vanessa Taylor, 1982

My daughter Vanessa and I are both ministers of the Gospel and the rapture will be good news to the ones living for Christ but bad news for those who live in sin. Vanessa loves to quote what the apostle Paul said "For the Lord, himself shall descend from heaven with a shout, with the voice of the archangel, and with the trumpet of God: and the dead in Christ shall rise first: Then we which are alive and remain shall be caught up together with them in the air; and so shall we ever be with the Lord" (Thess. 4:16&17). Vanessa knows she can't beat Jimmy (her brother) to meet the Lord in the air, but all of our loved ones in the grave who died in Christ we have the hope of meeting them very soon.

You would think all the people would have been convinced that Christ was the Messiah because of all the good news he brought, but some went and told the Pharisees who did not accept His message. The same thing holds true in the ministry of every believer. Some will believe you and others will not believe the good news, we can choose to go with Christ or Satan. Living for the devil allows you to abuse your bodies in many ways. Some illness is a result of our conduct, either knowingly or unknowing. Creation suffers sometimes because it is out of tune with its Creator. When we try to figure out illness of others we are falling into a trap set by Satan. We can only use the Word of God to find the way to restoration.

Illness is a state of the body when it is chemically out of balance. We may even become ill because the body is not properly cared for-from eating, rest, clothes, shelter. Abuses, such as smoking, drinking, and drugs may cause sickness. Some illnesses come by an invasion of a virus, a poison, germs or through accidents.

Sickness can sometimes be psychosomatic, caused by the spirit of man. Guilt, hate fear and other fruits of Satan can cause illness. The curse that is on the entire earth because of the original sin of Adam can cover all the other illnesses.

Healing is the process of recovery from illness to health. All healing comes from God, whether by the processes of nature, such as keeping a wound clean and free from infection, the wisdom that God gives to doctors and nurses, whether by the processes of nature or by miraculous healings as a result of prayer and faith. Regardless of the method, man must do his part by getting out of the way and letting God direct your path. God if allowed to, continues to heal us so we can serve Him. "Bless the Lord, O my soul... Who forgiveth all thine iniquities; who healeth all they diseases" (Psalm 103:2,3).

Healing was part of the benefits of Pentecost; Jesus has given believers the same benefits that David prophesied about in (Psalms 103). "They shall lay hands on the sick, and they shall recover" (Mark 16:18). Two things, the "prayer of faith" and "forgiveness of sin" (James 5:15) are the best things we benefit from. While unconfessed sin could block God's healing grace, the candidate for healing has God's assurance of forgiveness of sins.

The woman had "a spirit of infirmity." Which means she had a "weakness or sickness." According to Luke 13:16, which says, "ought not the women whom Satan hath bound be loosed on the Sabbath?" Luke goes on to say that she could not stand up straight. Demons have power. In Luke 13:12, they had physically bound a woman for eighteen years. However, Christ said, "Woman, thou art loosed from thine infirmity." The next verse says, she was "made straight," which is the Greek term "apolelusai." It meant, "to release" and was used in medicine in that day to indicate one's being released and put into a state of freedom. Christ's authority over demons is clear. The woman not only had a spiritual effect but a physical reality. She felt relieved in spirit and felt the physical effects of Christ's power over demon activity. James says, "devil's also believe, and trembles" (James 2:19). The demons no doubt trembled when Jesus laid his hands on this woman, and said, "woman thou art loosed from thine infirmity."

According to Matthew 25:41, "everlasting fire," is prepared for the devil and his angels." In Jude 6, the demons did not keep, "their first estate." They were originally angels created for good purposes, meant to serve God. They rebelled against God, and left this estate and became what we now know as demons. They do not fulfill the desires of God but pursue a realm outside of God. Demons are under the supreme authority of God. This supremacy and control is "everlasting." The rebellion is futile because demons are "reserved for sin everlasting chains" (Jude 6:6). This means they are "kept in custody." They are held in captivity and limited by our all powerful Savior. Although the demons are under the authority of Christ, they still are allowed to operate in the world. The demons are made subject to Christ and believers by the blood of Jesus (atonement), the name of Jesus and the Holy Spirit. Proof of this statement is found in Mt. 8:16-17; 12:28; Mk. 16:17; Acts 19:15 and many other places in God's word.

During the Tribulation described in Revelation, a war in heaven will take place. This war will result in getting rid of Satan and his demons from heaven. The time of rejoicing will be, when the Demons start their eternal sentence to punishment and torment in the Lake of fire, which will be their eternal sentence.

Demons were created with the other angels and they serve the purpose of evil. The Bible tells Christians that they can have victory over Demons. Demons are defeated by Christ. Through faith the Christians are free from the dominance of demons. The Christians have been given power over Demons, because Luke 10:19 says, any power they had was a power delegated from Him who has all power, both in heaven and in earth. I am so glad that Christ came into the world for the purpose of breaking Satan's power (Colossians 2:15) and to destroy his works (1 John 3:8).

PART V

Christ Our Resurrection

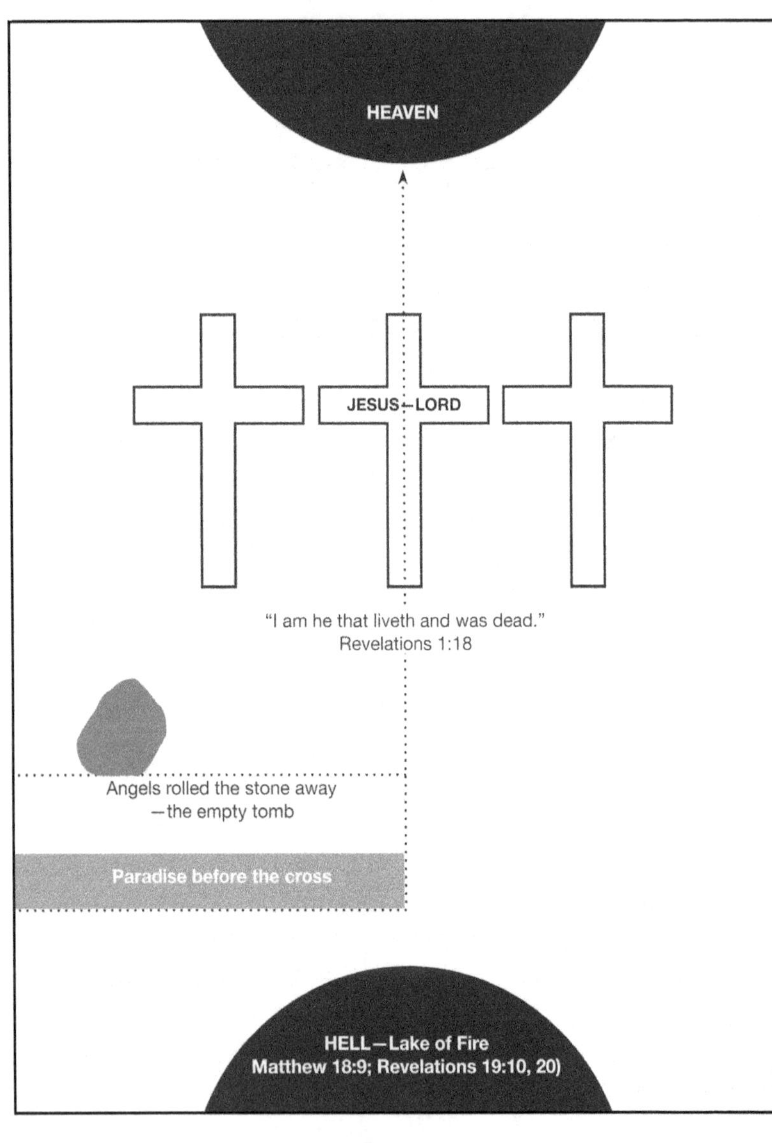
HEAVEN
JESUS—LORD
"I am he that liveth and was dead."
Revelations 1:18
Angels rolled the stone away
—the empty tomb
Paradise before the cross
HELL—Lake of Fire
Matthew 18:9; Revelations 19:10, 20)

AS WONDERFUL AS HIS RESURRECTION WAS, as Glorious as His return will be, neither would have occurred if He had not walked the lonesome road to Golgotha (John 19:17). Jesus was crucified between two criminals. Pilate and the ones crucifying Him didn't realize that prophecy was being fulfilled: "He was numbered with the transgressors" (Isaiah 53:12). He was also lifted up as Moses lifted up the serpent in the wilderness (Numbers 21:5-9). Jesus predicts His suffering and coming glory and He came forth as was His promise (Matthew 16:21; 20:19), and according to Paul Jesus arose and if He had not risen, then our faith would be in vain. We would yet be in our sins (1 Corinthians 15:17). Adam brought to us sin and death; Christ, through the resurrection, brought to us life (1 Corinthians 15:22).

"He which raised up the Lord Jesus shall raise up us also by Jesus (2 Corinthians 4:14). The phrase, "where of we all are witnesses" (Acts 2:32), first and most properly means the Twelve: but secondarily, the whole body of believers, all of whom, at this time, had probably seen the Lord since His resurrection. He proved his resurrection by appearing to many people, including an appearance to "above five hundred brethren at once." (1 Corinthians 15: 5-8). Jesus had said to the apostles, "But when the comforter is come, whom I will send unto you from the Father, even the Spirit of truth, which proceedeth from the Father, he shall testify of me: and ye also shall bear witness" (1 John 15:26,27). There, not only the apostles and the ones with the upper room experience, but the Holy Spirit which have experienced, also bears witness to those whom have received the Holy Spirit, up to this present time. The evidence which could be "seen" and "heard" bore witness that Jesus was not in the tomb, but was resurrected and had made it back to His Father. Wherever the Holy Spirit is poured out today, He is a witness to the resurrection and He is sent to glorify Christ.

Christ was crucified; second, Christ was raised from the dead; third, Christ is in heaven now, lifted up by the Father; and fourth, the Holy Spirit is here in His place and He lives in our bodies which is the Temple of the Holy Spirit (1 Corinthians 6:19). Salvation cannot be known apart from the confession of faith in the resurrection of Jesus Christ (Romans 10:9) ; "Our Savior Jesus Christ, ...hath abolished death, and hath brought life and immortality to light through the gospel" (2 Timothy 1:10). Christianity is the only faith on earth that gives assurance of life beyond the grave.

There are at least seven reasons given for Christ's resurrection: He arose because of what He is. Being the Eternal Son, it is not possible for death to hold him down (Acts 2:24); He arose because He is the Son of David, He must yet sit upon David's throne (Luke 1:31-33); He arose to be head over all of the church ; which is His body (Ephesians 1:22,23); He arose to be the giver of resurrection life (John 12:24); He arose to impart His resurrection power (Ephesians 1:19,20); He arose that sinners might be justified (Romans 4:25); and He arose that He might appear in Heaven as the pattern, or first fruits, of all who, being saved and conformed to Him, will yet appear with Him in glory (1 Corinthians 15:20-23).

Peter witnessed Jesus' resurrection: "This Jesus hath God raised up, whereof we all are witnesses" (Acts 2:32). Peter was very excited as he stood before this large crowd of people and his sermon centered on Jesus. He could speak from personal experience that Jesus died and God raised Him to Life. Peter also made it very clear that he was a witness to this resurrection of Jesus.

Christ's resurrection is a guarantee of others being resurrected according to Paul: "But now is Christ risen from the dead, and become the first fruits of them that slept. For since by man came death, by man came also the resurrection of the dead. For as in Adam all die, even so in Christ shall all be made alive. But every man in his own order. Christ the first fruits, afterward they that are Christ's at his coming" (1 Corinthians 15:20-23) . The last portion is us, Christians, who are here and alive when He wakes our loved ones who died in Christ, which is the mystery talked about in Verse 51. The resurrection is certain but there is some mystery about it. The mystery is that the Spiritual body don't die but the natural body dies.

Being set at the right hand of God indicates the position of power and authority that Jesus now holds. When Paul talks about the heavenly places (Ephesians 1:20), he indicates the presence of God and the dominion of His Kingdom over the world.

The principalities and powers (Verse 21), refer to several realities. First, it means the spiritual powers that exercise dominion over the earth as they ruled from the atmosphere. Second, it is often used today to refer to institutional powers of governments and economic systems that abuse people. The apostle Paul tells of the Holy Ghost power which works for the good of people and is "for believers, not unbelievers" (Ephesians 1:19).

Nothing in this world should be allowed to control the life of the believer other than the Lordship of Jesus Christ. Jesus has been established as the victorious King of Kings and Lord of Lords by the mighty act of God.

The reference to "every name that is named" reminds us of Philippians 2:9-11: "Wherefore, God also hath exalted him, and given him a name which is above every name; That at the name of Jesus every Knee should bow, of things in heaven, and things in earth, and things under the earth, and that every tongue should confess that Jesus Christ is Lord, to the glory of God, the Father."

Also Ephesians 1:21-23 shows the authority and the dominion that the exalted Christ has. "Far above all principality and power and might, and dominion, and every name that is named, not only in this world, but also in that which is to come: And hath put all things under his feet, and gave him to be the head over all things to the church Which is his body the fullness of him that filleth all in all."

These verses clearly show us the Victory of Jesus over the world. The victory that all Christians should show they have in Christ over this world. The first part of verse 22 is from Psalm 8:6: "Thou madest him to have dominion over the works of thy hands; thou hast put all things under his feet." This is another way of expressing the fact that His enemies have become His footstool and He uses them to rest upon.

We can have resurrection life down here if we believe on Christ. We are just pilgrims and strangers down here on earth but we Christians are citizens of the Kingdom of God. When these principles by which Christians live by go into action we will experience a freedom to witness with power, thanks to Jesus Christ.

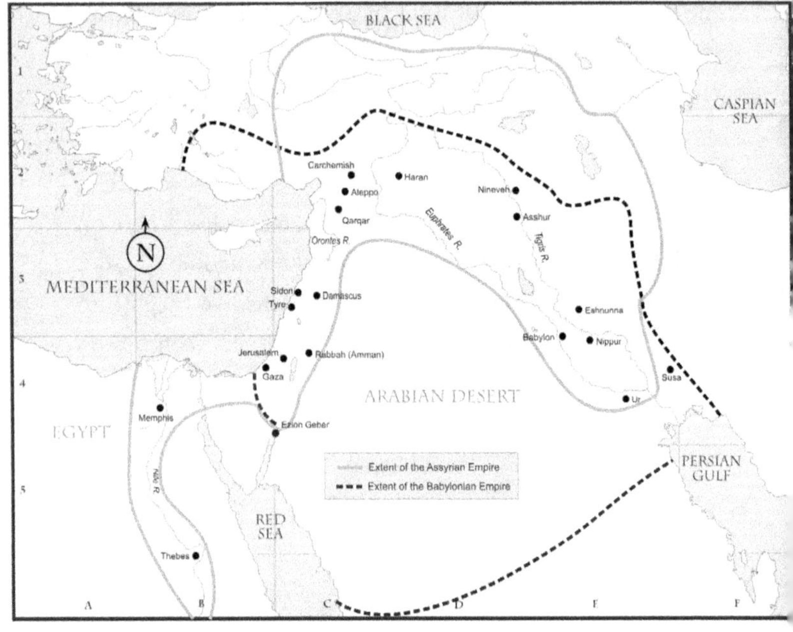

The Satanic Trinity portrayed by Rev. C.C. Gosey helps me to explain my thoughts on the "Scarlet Woman," which I believe will represent the World Church and has the Eastern Division of the Greek Church as one leg and the Western Division of the Papal Church as the other leg. I believe the Scarlet Woman will put these legs around the Beast and ride to the future world capital Babylon to worship the Beast and she will ride on the Beast to Jerusalem.

After three and a half years into the tribulation, mystery Babylon (the religious system) worships the antichrist and He will rule from the world capital (rebuilt city of Babylon) until the King of kings and Lord of lords comes to rule and reign in the new Jerusalem.

PART VI

THE ANTICHRIST

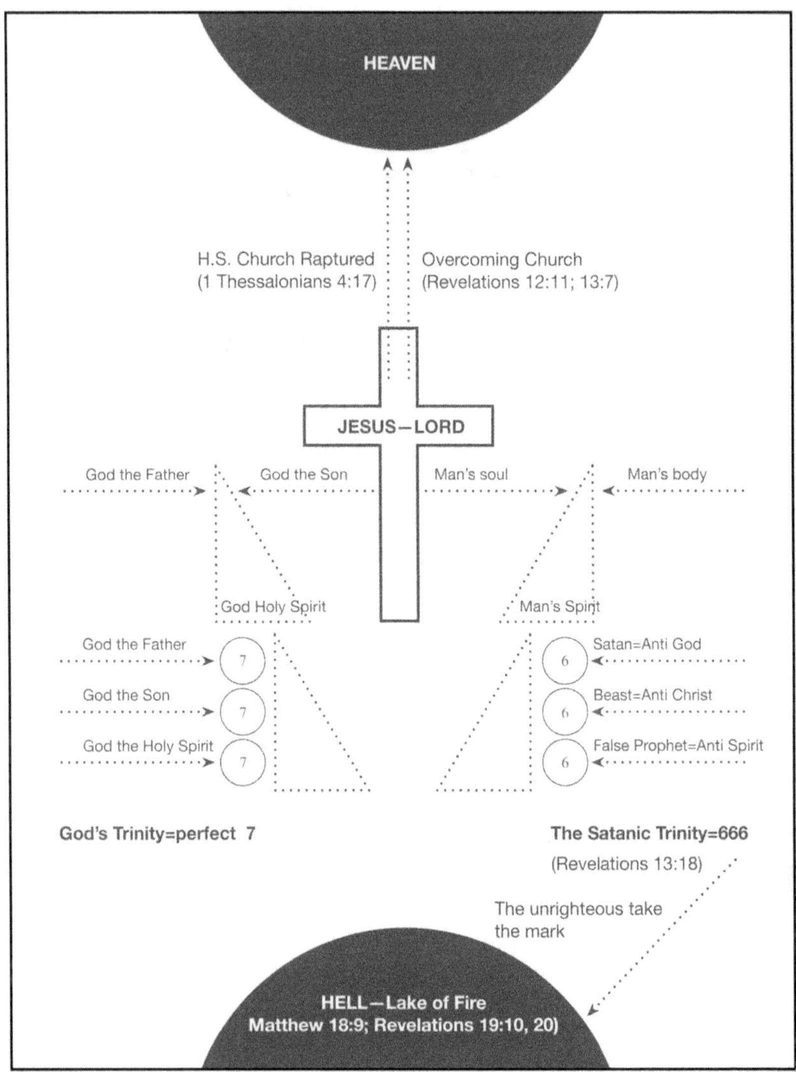
HEAVEN
H.S. Church Raptured
(1 Thessalonians 4:17)
Overcoming Church
(Revelations 12:11; 13:7)
JESUS—LORD
God the Father
God the Son
Man's soul
Man's body
God Holy Spirit
Man's Spirit
God the Father
God the Son
God the Holy Spirit
7
7
7
Satan=Anti God
Beast=Anti Christ
False Prophet=Anti Spirit
6
6
6
God's Trinity=perfect 7
The Satanic Trinity=666
(Revelations 13:18)
The unrighteous take
the mark
HELL—Lake of Fire
Matthew 18:9; Revelations 19:10, 20)

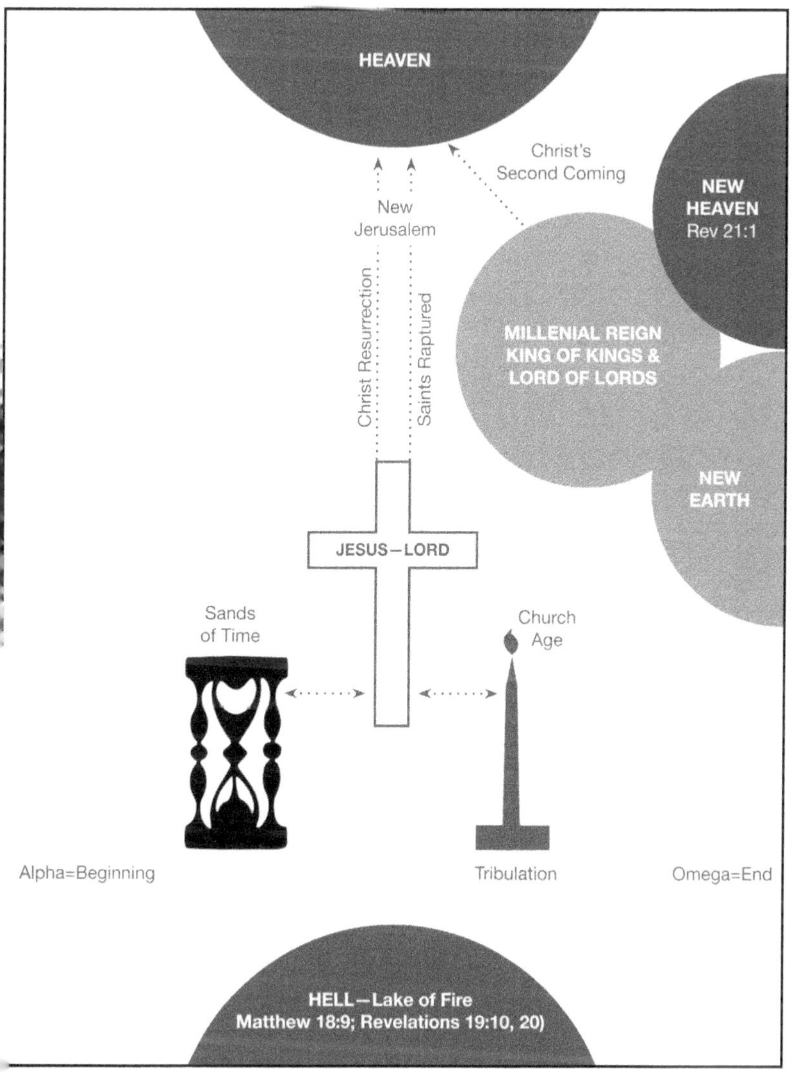
HEAVEN
Christ's
Second Coming
New
Jerusalem
Christ Resurrection
Saints Raptured
NEW
HEAVEN
Rev 21:1
MILLENIAL REIGN
KING OF KINGS &
LORD OF LORDS
NEW
EARTH
JESUS—LORD
Sands
of Time
Church
Age
Alpha=Beginning
Tribulation
Omega=End
HELL—Lake of Fire
Matthew 18:9; Revelations 19:10, 20)

THE BIBLE FORETELLS A PERIOD of great tribulation when a world dictator will rule the earth. "They have no rest day nor night, who worship the beast and his image, and whoever received the mark of his name" (Revelation 14:11).

The antichrist will worship the devil, and he will cause all those under him to worship the devil. The power of the antichrist will make him a very attractive person. Men will adore him, and receive him (John 5:43). One translation reads: "and the whole earth went after the beast in amazement and admiration." The masses will turn to the worship of the beast (antichrist) and of the dragon (Satan) who will empower him. Not the creator, but Satan will become the object of universal worship. Not only will Satan be worshipped, but the beast will also be worshipped, which will be a universal worship. (Revelation 13:4).

The antichrist will set himself up as the only God and will demand worship of the peoples of the earth (Daniel 11:30). Paul said, that the man of sin "opposeth and exaleth himself above all that is called God, or that is worshipped, so that he as God sitteth in the temple of God, showing himself that he is God" (2 Thessalonians 2:4). The antichrist will not be operating in his own power, but in the power of Satan. He will be under the control of the devil (Revelation 13:7).

Those who stand for Christ will be hated by the antichrist. Satan will not have the power to force the saints of God to worship him and the only ones who will worship and follow him are those whose names are not found written in the Book of Life. The redeemed of God can never be touched by Satan. The beast will conquer and kill, but eternal life will be given to the martyrs, which are the ones that have given allegiance to God.

In order for everyone on earth to know that they are giving allegiance to him as God, the antichrist will make them take the mark of the beast in their right hands or in their foreheads. Six is the number of a man; it is a falling short of the biblical perfect number seven. It will be the number of man: 666, a triple falling away (Revelation 13:16-18).

It's amazing to me that Christ's birth was foretold, His kingdom, conquest of the antichrist and the antichrist name was given to us (Micah 5:1-6). Micah lived hundreds of years before Christ or the antichrist will live on earth. The prophet said his name would be the Assyrian (Micah 5:5&6) and would be the antichrist when the peace which is Christ the prince of peace shall come in to deliver them. Notice that the word Assyrian is singular which refers to the antichrist and not Assyrians as a people.

He is called the Assyrian because he will come from the territory Assyria ruled over in ancient times (Micah 5:5). For this same reason he can be called the King of Babylon (Isaiah 14). The Syrian (Daniel 11:35-45). The Roman prince that shall come (Daniel 9:26-27), and the Grecian (Zech. 9:13). He will come from the territory ruled by Assyria at the time of these prophecies which included Babylon, Greece, Syria and Rome. In the days of Isaiah the Assyrians had the great empire of Bible lands, so the future antichrist should rightly be called the Assyrian. The Assyrians in the days of Isaiah, and Hezekiah did not tread in palaces of Judah, so this treading refers to that of the future antichrist when he will take over all of Palestine, Jerusalem, and even the future Jewish temple at Jerusalem (Daniel 9:27; 11:40-45; Matthew 24:15, Revelation 11:1-2).

"We must put on the whole armour of God" (Ephesians 6:11-17)." Try without God and you will lose every battle but with God we will win over sin. Many men have yielded their facilities to a life of sin and Satan who is not only active himself but uses these yielded instruments. No one, however has been so totally dominated by him as will be the final world dictator known as the antichrist. Satan will work his will through this person. He will exercise great power over men, and Satan will turn his power over to the antichrist. He will attempt but fail to prevent the triumph of Christ. John saw this Beast come out of the sea, the sea means arise from out of the people, and it was a monstrous Beast. It had leopard like figures, and had some characteristics of a bear and a lion. This description is in Revelation 13:1,2.

The Beast who represented the antichrist got its power and throne and authority from the dragon who represented Satan. The antichrist will be committed to fulfill the devil's desire in the fullness of time. I have seen several men arise in recent years but each of these men has had a limited following from a limited and restricted location. But the Bible gives us a different picture of the antichrist.

Men from every corner of the whole world will follow the antichrist. This will be more than a political connection because they will worship him. They will admire him so much that they will even worship the devil as the source of the antichrist's power and charm.

In the fullness of time, for a period of time, God will be set aside and the antichrist will be worshipped in His place. Throughout history men have forgotten the true source of their help but there never has been a time on earth like that day when men transfer their affections away from God.

The antichrist will show an arrogant attitude in exercising his authority. His speech will be proud and blasphemous. This cold-hearted authority of the Beast is found in Revelation 13:5-7. This evil one will blaspheme those who live in heaven. The saints can be persecuted and murdered without a cry for help being raised, we sometimes hear of someone being attacked while a crowd of people look on and do nothing. This kind of attitude will cover the whole world under the reign of the antichrist. He will exercise authority over people worldwide and none will come to aid those who resist him.

It is so hard for me to believe the ability that the antichrist will have to sway people and to capture their affections and trust. Men from all walks of life and from all over the world will bow before him as though he were God. It is a frightening thought that the educated, the elite, the rich, the powerful, the illiterate, the castaways, the poor, the helpless, will bow down and worship the antichrist.

The tribulation saints who resist him, whose names have been written in the Book of Life, will be able to pay by laying down their lives for the Lord. His grace will sustain those who trust in Him. The Lord will have a few saints that will give their life before bowing to this man of great influence (Revelation 13:8-15).

This Beast's (Revelation 13:11-15) allegiance will be to the antichrist and he will entice men everywhere to worship Him. He will have the capacity to perform great and mighty miracles including causing fire to come down from heaven in view of everybody. He will even set up an image of the first beast, cause it to speak, and kill all of those who refuse to worship the image. The saints of God have faced many things in times past but nothing will compare with this time which will come.

The place of the mark starts in Revelation 13:16: " and he causeth all, both small and great, rich and poor, free and bond, to receive a mark in their right hand, or in their foreheads." This beast will force all men to identify with the antichrist by receiving his mark in their right hand or in their forehead.

Without this mark according to (Revelation 13:17), you can't buy or sell without the mark. "And that no man might buy or sell, save he that had the mark, or the name of the beast, or the number of his name.

This meant that they cannot buy land, or a house, or clothes, or food, or sell anything. Only the people who are trusting the Lord can resist taking the mark. All of those who take the mark sell their souls eternally to Satan.

The battle between good and evil and his defeat is found in Revelation 19: 19-21. The battle between Christ and Satan, good and bad, right and wrong has been going on since the fall of Lucifer. Ever since Adam sinned, man has been struggling with good and evil. The battle rages, but the ultimate victory is ours, our confidence and trust rests in our all powerful God who will reward us with Heaven eternal but the consequences of wrongdoing is found in verse 20 of chapter 19: "And the beast was taken, and with him the false prophet that wrought miracles before him, with which he deceived them that had received the mark of the beast, and them that worshipped his image. These both were cast alive into a lake of fire burning with brimstone."

The antichrist and the False prophet (The second beast) will be successful and seen to be invincible, but when they face Christ and His armies, they will be no match for Him. The Lord could stop these wicked rulers at any point, but he will always wait for the fullness of time.

When the fullness of time comes, He will take the antichrist and the False prophet and throw them alive into the Lake of Fire. Their end will be anything but beautiful and will last for eternity. By warning men of the consequences of sin, we may save them from this eternal pain. Sin does not pay and it is fatal because everyone who followed the antichrist and false prophet suffered their eternal punishment. Christ has all the power, the power to save and the power to punish eternally because He gives final judgment to all men whether ours deeds are good or bad, we will be held accountable for them, and we will be judged or rewarded accordingly, Jesus declared Himself to be the judge. He said, "For the Father judgeth no man, but hath committed all judgment into the Son" (John 5:22). "Jesus said, When the Son of man shall come in his glory, and all the holy angels with him, then shall he sit up on the throne of his glory"

(Matthew 24:31). He who has been the source of grace and mercy will occupy the seat of judgment. Those who reject Jesus Christ as Savior must one day face Him as their judge.

PART VII

THE END

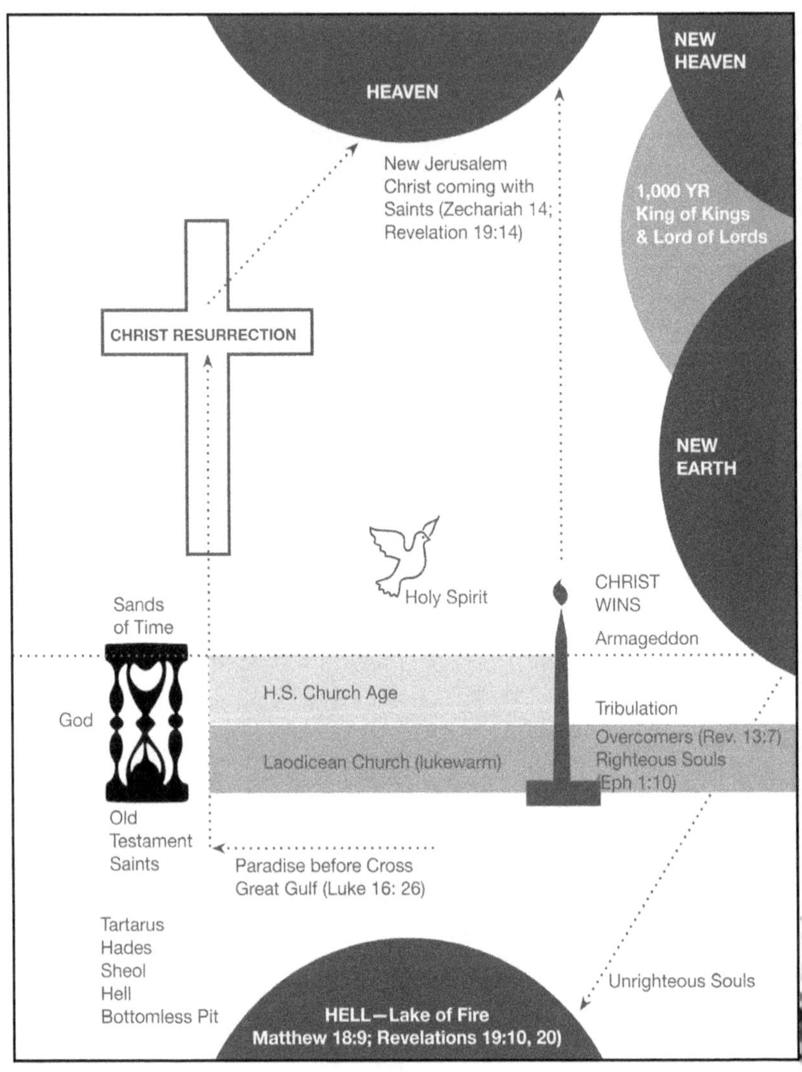
HEAVEN
NEW HEAVEN
New Jerusalem
Christ coming with
Saints (Zechariah 14;
Revelation 19:14)
1,000 YR
King of Kings
& Lord of Lords
CHRIST RESURRECTION
NEW EARTH
Holy Spirit
CHRIST
WINS
Armageddon
Sands
of Time
H.S. Church Age
Tribulation
God
Laodicean Church (lukewarm)
Overcomers (Rev. 13:7)
Righteous Souls
(Eph 1:10)
Old
Testament
Saints
Paradise before Cross
Great Gulf (Luke 16: 26)
Tartarus
Hades
Sheol
Hell
Bottomless Pit
Unrighteous Souls
HELL—Lake of Fire
Matthew 18:9; Revelations 19:10, 20)

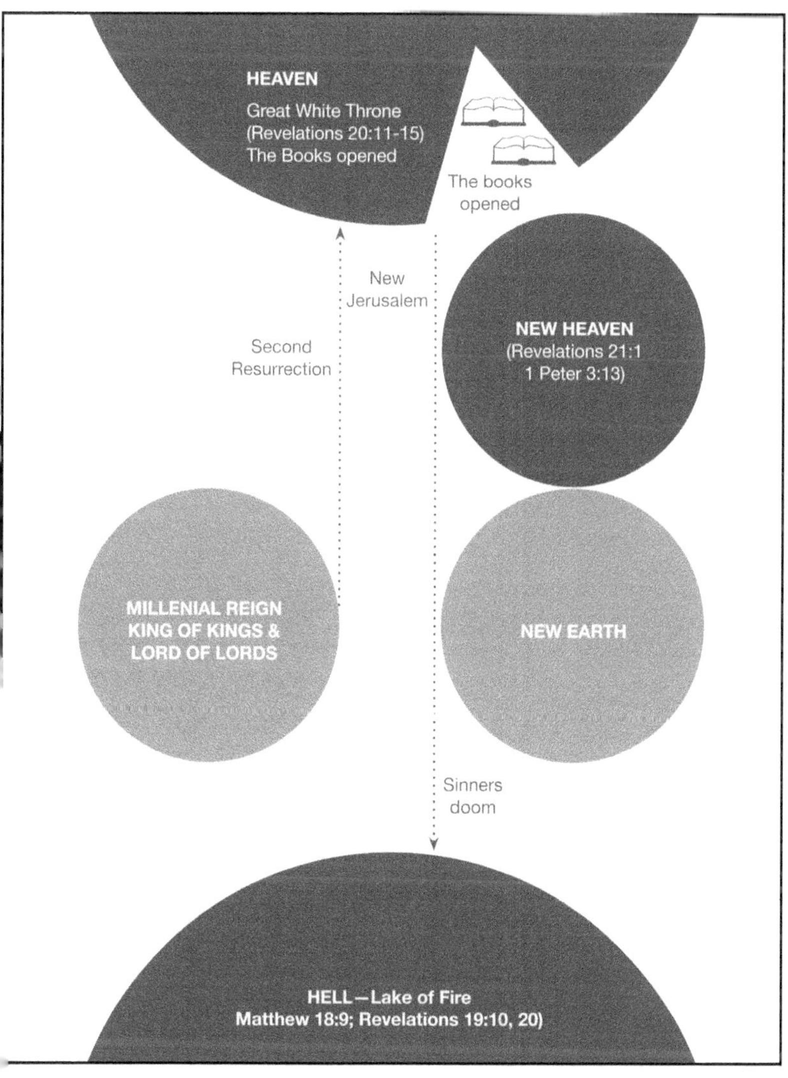
HEAVEN
Great White Throne
(Revelations 20:11-15)
The Books opened
The books
opened
New
Jerusalem
Second
Resurrection
NEW HEAVEN
(Revelations 21:1
1 Peter 3:13)
MILLENIAL REIGN
KING OF KINGS &
LORD OF LORDS
NEW EARTH
Sinners
doom
HELL—Lake of Fire
Matthew 18:9; Revelations 19:10, 20)

JESUS CLAIMED, that He was the resurrection and the life (John 11:25) and that he held the Keys of both life and death (Revelation 1:18).

The "first resurrection" is in several phases: the resurrection of Christ as the beginning of the first resurrection (1 Corinthians 15:23) ; the resurrection of the saints who died during the Church age together with the transformation of the livery saints commonly called the Rapture (1 Thessalonians 4:16), and the resurrection of the faithful during the Tribulation. The unrighteous dead will have no part in this first resurrection, for their destiny will come forth at the end of the millennium.

Each of us has a master here on earth and our lifestyle shows who is in charge. If we serve sin, we are servants of Satan but if we are servants of righteousness, we practice obedience to Christ, and we will live in God's righteous Kingdom forever. If we serve sin, we will live in Hell forever.

We get to choose where we want to dwell forever. We should choose and practice obedience to Christ, because He purchased us with His own Life's blood at Calvary. The righteousness Christ has produced in our hearts will cause us to live right and act right. The final result will be eternal life.

The apostle Paul said, "That ye might walk worthy of the Lord unto all pleasing, being fruitful in every good work, and increasing in the knowledge of God" (Colossians 1:10).

Paul speaks of two gifts God gives to believers: (I) redemption through His precious blood (II) forgiveness of sins. If we allow the Lord to redeem us, He sets us free from the bondage of sin and then we belong to Him and we are not only freed from the bondage of sin but also its guilt. We who were prisoners and servants of sin, were living under the sentence of everlasting death, can now praise God, that Christ set us free from the curse of sin and death.

The Christians final result will be eternal life. "But now being made free from sin, and become servants to God, ye have your fruit unto holiness, and the end everlasting life" (Romans 6:22). Before the Christian gave their lives to God, they were on the road to eternal death which is the product of the sin controlled life.

The apostle Paul says believers should thank God, because we have been set free from Satan's control and been delivered and caused to stand. "Who hath delivered us from the power of darkness, and hath translated us into the kingdom of his dear Son: In whom we have redemption through his blood, even the forgiveness of sins."

The Spirit and soul of man lives forever. The grave is only a temporary place where man passes in order to reach the life beyond. His future is determined by the personal choice and attitude of the soul toward the atoning work of the Lord Jesus Christ.

Death is a period of dread for the unregenerate person but a time of joy because of the promise of the eternal life with the Lord for the Christian. When Christ arose at the resurrection, He conquered all and the believers' future state was assured. "But if the Spirit of him that raised up Jesus from the dead dwell in you, he that raised up Christ from the dead shall also quicken your mortal bodies by his Spirit that dwelleth in you" (Romans 8:11).

Jesus gave us a picture of a rich man who lived only for himself and a poor beggar who had nothing. They both died and it can be assumed that Lazareth was a servant of God because he was taken to Abraham's bosom. The rich man was in a place of punishment where he is in torment according to Luke 16:23: "And in hell he lifted up his eyes, being in torments, and seeth Abraham afar off, and Lazarus in his bosom."

Christ by the offering of Himself has made a perfect atonement for sin and has thus destroyed the power of sin, death, and the devil. We all still have the appointment of natural death but it has lost its sting for all who believe and receive Christ as Savior.

Jesus Christ has done away with death and brought eternal life to those who accept Christ as their Savior. To the ones who don't accept Christ there is Death. Death is the separation of soul and body, which takes us to the unseen world. This is described as sleep in John 11:11 and Deuteronomy 31:16. In the parable of the rich fool, God had a right and the power to say "this night thy soul be required of thee" (Luke 12:20). I want to always be ready for life or death, so I can say what the apostle Paul said, "For me to live is Christ, and to die is gain."

God made man in His image. God has to exist in Heaven forever and Satan must exist in Hell forever. We all have a life to live, a death to die, judgment to face, an eternity to enjoy in heaven or a hell to endure eternally.

The wrath of God will be poured out upon the ones that miss the rapture, they will have to see the following because of disobedience: the moon and stars fall, the sun will be darkened, the mountains will crumble, when Jesus comes back with His Spirit-filled Church terrible things will happen.

God has always taken His children or has given them a chance to get away before He pours His wrath out. Drinking of the living water is mentioned which is the symbol of the Holy Spirit. Since the Holy Spirit church is going on the first load to Heaven. The "Holy Spirit and the bride are saying, whosoever will, let him take of the water of life freely" (Rev. 22:17). These are the last words Jesus spoke to close the Holy Ghost Dispensation and will return to the Old Testament System with His people, the Jews. The Jews will be grafted back into the tree; since the Holy Ghost church was born on the Day of Pentecost.

The Beast makes war with the Saints, and to overcomes them (Rev. 13:7). "And all that dwell upon the earth (the Holy Ghost church has been taken before the antichrist is revealed) shall worship him, whose names are not written in the Book of Life of the Lamb slain from the foundation of the world. The remainder of Revelation 13 tells of the Satanic trinity which tries to duplicate God the Father (Anti-God), God the Son (antichrist-beast) and the False Prophet (anti-spirit-World Church tries to duplicate the Holy Spirit). The false prophet will deceive by calling fire down from heaven and the antichrist gives life to the image of the beast.

Then he causes the great, the rich, and poor free and bond, to receive a mark (666) in their right hand or in their forehead (Revelation 13:13-18).

For the end to come, we need revival, because the gospel must be preached to all the world (Matthew 24:14). All who do not receive Christ before His first coming (Rapture) will have to go through seven years of tribulation. Many will have to give their lives for Christ and obey His word to be ready when He comes with His Saints and wins the battle of Armageddon.

According to the Word His first coming (Rapture) is very soon, because all of the signs have been fulfilled. Christ tells us in (Matthew 24:32-34) that we should know how to "discern the signs of the times." The fig tree in verses (32-34) represents Israel and all the trees, the Gentiles.This Scripture says, we are to learn this parable "Now learn a parable of the fig tree; when his branch is yet tender" This is Israel in 1948, when it became a young tender nation. When her people came back from all over the earth, which signifies the leaves ("ye know that summer is nigh: So likewise ye, when ye shall see all these things, know that it is near, even at the doors") This is the sign of the times Matthew 24 speaks about.

In Matt. 24:34, He says, verily I say unto you, this generation shall not pass, till all these things be fulfilled. His children know the signs of time in Matt 24:14, and they know that summer is nigh" and "are not in darkness." The word says, "But ye brethren, are not in darkness, that day should overtake you as a thief" (1 Thess. 5:1-5)

The fig tree in Matthew 24:32 is the symbol of the Nation of Israel. The summer is the end of the age. The word "summer" in the Hebrew means "end." The tree (Israel) has been very tender since Israel became a Nation in 1948 and is now putting forth leaves, so we know "summer is near." The Jews (leaves) have been returning to Israel (the tree) from every nation since 1948.

Israel became a nation one year after I invited Jesus into my heart. The Bible says, (Thessalonians 5:1-5) the generation that saw this happen (the star of David fly in Israel) would not all die until all be fulfilled. So I believe Jesus Christ will come for His children (Rapture) to take us to Heaven, before all my generation dies.

The rapture is when He comes for His Saints that are looking for him and are ready to go. Also according to (Rev. 19:11-16) he comes with His saints to the battle of Armageddon. (Zech 14) tells about in that battle, all nations will go to battle against Israel, but Christ wins! His "feet will stand on the Mt. of Olives" (Zech 14:4), where He rose (Acts 1:9) and angels told His disciples (Acts 1:11) that HE would return in the same manner."

Jews, I urge you to flee to Petra (City of Rock) and Jesus will "nourish" you during the Great Tribulation until He comes for you. The rock city (Isa. 2:10) is where the Jews need to flee, when the antichrist breaks his peace agreement with them and this starts the Great Tribulation. You will need to stay there for three and a half years, at which time Jesus Christ will "nourish" you until He comes for you.

The proud will be humbled and everyone will exalt God there in the city of Petra. The Bible says, God has prepared this place for you and all who goes and obeys God, will be fed by an eagle (Jere. 4-14, Deut. 32:11-14, Prov. 30:18-19). Some say, this could be the U.S. that God will use, or it could be a bird, like the raven. He used to feed the Prophet Elijah. For those of you that don't make it in the rapture please go to Petra and compel everyone to go with you to this City of Rock.

I personally know that Petra exists because I rode a horse back among those cliffs until we came to Petra. It is a ruby red rock, with pillars and a opening into this City of Rock. They told me in 1979, when I visited Israel, that the Holy Bibles were coated with cosmoline like you coat (firearms) to preserve them there.

It will be a humbling experience for you to go through this rough terrain, but this will save your life, and save your soul, when you obey your Messiah during these horrible times of the Great Tribulation.

In 1978 Don headed for Petra.

The Word of God says we can overcome Satan "by the blood of the lamb" and "by the word of our testimony." Also with His seal on our forehead, this protects us because this seal is greater than the antichrist's mark 666. I also believe that just before Christ comes for the Jewish people that the Prophet (one being Elijah) will bring a revival to the Nation of Israel. Israel will then accept their Messiah and HE will be their Savior and will become King of Kings and Lord of Lords forever to them, and all who were watching and waiting to make Heaven their eternal home.

According to Revelation 7:4, "one hundred and forty-four thousand of all the tribes of the children of Israel were sealed." Just before the second coming of Jesus which will be near the end of the Tribulation, one third of the ones who have survived will be saved (Zech. 13:9).

At the end of the Tribulation, which will be at the end of the war, at the second coming, Jesus will bring peace to the whole world. Jesus will set up His Kingdom and Jesus will be the King of Kings and Lord of Lords.

The Prophet Isaiah speaks of a lasting peace (Isa. 2:2-4). "In the last days" during the 1,000 year reign, Jesus will rule all nations, then there will be peace at last. "And they shall beat their swords into pruninghooks; nation shall not lift up sword against nation, neither shall they learn war any more."

There was peace in the Garden of Eden before the sin of man. The root of the Jews and Arabs hatred (sin) one toward the other has been going on thirty-five hundred years, but their sinful hearts can be washed in the blood of the lamb (whose blood is Christ Jesus' our Lord and Savior).

When Jesus comes into their lives, then they will have peace just like Adam and Eve had before sin entered the Garden of Eden. I have experienced what Jesus did for me! He took my hate, put it into the sea of forgetfulness and gave me love for everybody.

Christ came into my heart in the late fall of 1947. The first black person came to our school in that year by the name of Sammy. When the Lord saved me, we became best friends and protected each other until we earned the other students respect, by playing games and showing respect for them.

I was like all the rest of the students and wanted to conform and be like everybody else, but when Jesus saved me, He put love in my heart for Sammy. We then saw each other as a person and not as a different race. The color of a face or a different race wasn't what caused Jesus to shed His blood, because He died so the whole world could be saved.

Before the Prince of Peace comes (His 2nd coming) (Zechariah 14:2). All nations will come to battle against Israel and in (II Thessalonians 1:8-10) God's future judgment will be poured out. "In flaming fire, taking vengeance on them that know not God, and that obey not the Gospel of our Lord Jesus Christ: who shall be punished with everlasting destruction from the presence of the Lord, and from the glory of His power; when He shall come to be glorified in His Saints, and to be admired in all them that believe (because our testimony among you was believed).

In the Old Testament the Holy Ghost moved upon the Prophets, Priests, and Kings. During the Church Age or Holy Ghost dispensation, which started on the Day of Pentecost, when the church was born, the Holy Spirit now works through individual members of the Body of Christ.

These individual members invite the Holy Spirit to come into their bodies and dwell, which becomes the Temple of the Holy Spirit. We are very blessed to have the privilege of inviting the sweet Holy Ghost to dwell inside of us, Christians.

I believe during the tribulation the 144,000 Evangelists, martyred Saints and the two Prophets of Revelation 11, will have the Holy Spirit come upon them for special tasks, just as He did in the O.T. times prior to the Day of Pentecost.

When Christ died on the cross, He paid the debt for the sins of the whole world. We all have a choice to receive Him as our Savior or allow Satan to take us to the lake of fire, where he is going. In this Holy Ghost Dispensation, He has sent the Holy Ghost to lead us into all truth. He said if we would ask for the Comforter, we would receive Him, seek and we would find, knock and it shall be opened.

Jesus "will give of the fountain of the water of life freely to him who thirsts" (Revelation 21:6-7). He also said in this scripture, "he who overcomes shall inherit all things, and I will be his God and he shall be my son." God also refers to Himself as the "Alpha and the Omega, and The Beginning and The End."

In the Kingdom of God everything begins and ends in Jerusalem. When the New Jerusalem comes down out of Heaven, this will be the home of God and man (Revelation 21:2-3; 21:10). I believe the Capitol of the New Heaven and New Earth will be New Jerusalem, simply because the King of Kings and the Lord of Lords will rule all the world from there.

I know that the dwelling place of the righteous, of course is, "In my Father's House in Heaven" (John 14:2-3), but we will live with Christ 1,000 years on the New Earth and it's center will be where Christ rules and reigns during this time. God will have the New Heaven and New Earth for the Saints to live in and God will live with us forever and ever...Praise God!

I can't hardly wait for the time of the "hereafter" in Heaven but "The things which shall be hereafter" (Revelation 4:1) on earth, I want no part of it. I plan to go in the rapture at this time and the Bible says, the Heavenly Temple and a door was opened for the raptured saints with God (4:1-5:14). I believe "the four and twenty Elder" that fell down to worship are the twelve disciples and twelve Apostles. The redeemed, the Heavenly Angels and all the Heavenly Hosts will fall down before the throne and worship God. There will be Universal worship of Christ the Lamb of God, according to (Revelation 5:13) "every creature" worships Him which is in Heaven and on the earth.

During this same time the antichrist will come forth on the earth for people to bow down and worship him. You can look at the Roman Empire Map or The Empire Map of Alexander the Great and find the area which was then known as the whole world. The Bible lets us know where the legs, the "ten toes," and "the ten horns of the image were located." Rome was the legs of iron and the feet of clay and iron on Nebuchadnezzar's image. However, instead of having ten toes, this beast had ten horns. They represent ten nations that will reign just before God sets up His Kingdom.

The Eastern Division of the Greek Church is one leg of the image which Daniel saw and the Western Division of the Papal Church is the other leg which are the way this image moves around. I believe the Scarlet Woman will put these legs around the beast and ride. The "ten toes" of the image represents Ten Federated Kingdoms (in the above area) during the tribulation period. You will find the territory of the Western Division and the Papal Church originally grew from the Empire of Alexander the Great and the Roman Empire Maps which are included in this book. The ten horns which are spoken of in Daniel7:7 are included in these two empires.

The Assyrian (little horn) in Daniel 7:8 will be from the Assyrian Empire territory, This little horn is the antichrist and I feel we should know the place where he comes from. We know the ones that go in the rapture won't know who he is but we know his nationality because the Bible tells us (Micah 5:5-6; Dan. 7:8; Isa. 10:5; Gen. 10:8-12). Neither will we know the day or hour of the rapture, but we know the season. We only know that "summer" which is harvest is nigh because of the leaves (Jews) on the tree (Israel) are coming from all over the world because the nation of Israel now exists. We also know that "summer" is harvest time in Israel.

The last world ruler, the Assyrian, will be possessed by the same spirit as Nimrod, the first world ruler. The Assyrian will rule the whole world and everyone will worship him. Nimrod was from the line of Noah. He traveled to the plain, in the land of Shinar (Babylon) which means two rivers, one was the Euphrates River and the other the Tigris River.

They wanted to build the Tower of Babel to Heaven to make a name for themselves and to prevent dispersion over the earth, as God had commanded them to do. Both reasons for building this "City of Man" and Tower was against God's plan and the Lord fixed it so it was impossible to complete by confounding their language (Gen. 11:1-9). God will allow the antichrist to rebuild the city of Babylon, but will destroy it after the Tribulation, when Christ wins the war of Armageddon.

Just prior to this war, the Beast makes war with the Saints and overcomes them (Rev. 13:7). "And all that dwell upon the earth shall worship him, whose names are not written in the book of life of the Lamb slain from the foundation of the world." There will be many "overcomers" that will be slain before they would take this mark of the Satanic trinity (666). The remainder of Revelation 13 tells about the Satanic Trinity trying to duplicate God the Father (Anti God), God the Son (The Beast-antichrist) and the False Prophet (Anti Spirit-World Church) tries to duplicate the Holy Spirit.

Satan with his Anti-God, antichrist and Anti-Spirit has tried to destroy everything that God has created but will end up himself in eternal fire. God made man in His image which is body, soul and spirit. God has to exist in Heaven forever and Satan's future home is in the lake of fire forever. We all have a life to live, a death to die, a choice of who we follow home (Satan or God), judgment to face, and eternity to endure in Heaven or in Hell on into The Lake of Fire that burns forever.

I believe with all my heart the signs of the time, to fulfill the Holy Spirit Dispensation, will soon be fulfilled. When we have obeyed The Great Commission (Matthew 28:19-20) and "Teaching them to observe all things whatsoever I have commanded you : lo, I am with you always, even to the end of the world". The Lord gave us this commission and this command (Acts 1:8) before He takes His Holy Spirit Church in the Rapture.

Every Nation in the whole world must hear the Gospel and receive Jesus' command that HE made just before He was taken up to Heaven to be with His heavenly Father. The ones that obey and receive the power (Acts 1:8) and endure to the end shall make Heaven their Home when Jesus comes for them.

The present Church of today is The Laodicean Church. This church is the Lukewarm, self satisfied one. Our Lord said in Revelation 3:16, "I will spew thee out of my mouth." This word spew means to spit out with force-or vomit, but this lukewarm Church won't "hear what the Spirit saith unto the churches." In the very next verse (Rev. 4:1) the rapture takes place and He tells of things "which must be hereafter."

Our Lord and Savior gives each one a choice to "hear what the Spirit saith unto the churches," but has so much love for us that if we choose not to listen to Him, He will allow us His Children to stay here and go through the Great Tribulation (Revelation 7:14) by being an overcomer. Those saints who go through the great tribulation will hunger, thirst and cry but "God Himself shall wipe away all tears from their eyes." All of God's children will have spiritual fullness in the fullness of time!

* * * * * *

Jews, I urge you to flee to Petra (City of Rock) and Jesus will "nourish" you during the Great Tribulation until he comes for you. The rock city (Isa. 2:10) is where the Jews need to flee, when the anti-christ breaks his peace agreement with them and this starts the Great Tribulation. You will need to stay there for three and a half years, at which time Jesus Christ will "nourish" you until He comes for you.

Wake up world! Jesus is coming soon! Read about the anti-christ "mark" in Rev. 13:16-17. Also search the internet for possible implantable devices and you will see the end of time is near. T.D. Jakes has very good advice: "Get ready - get ready - get ready!"

—Don Brewer

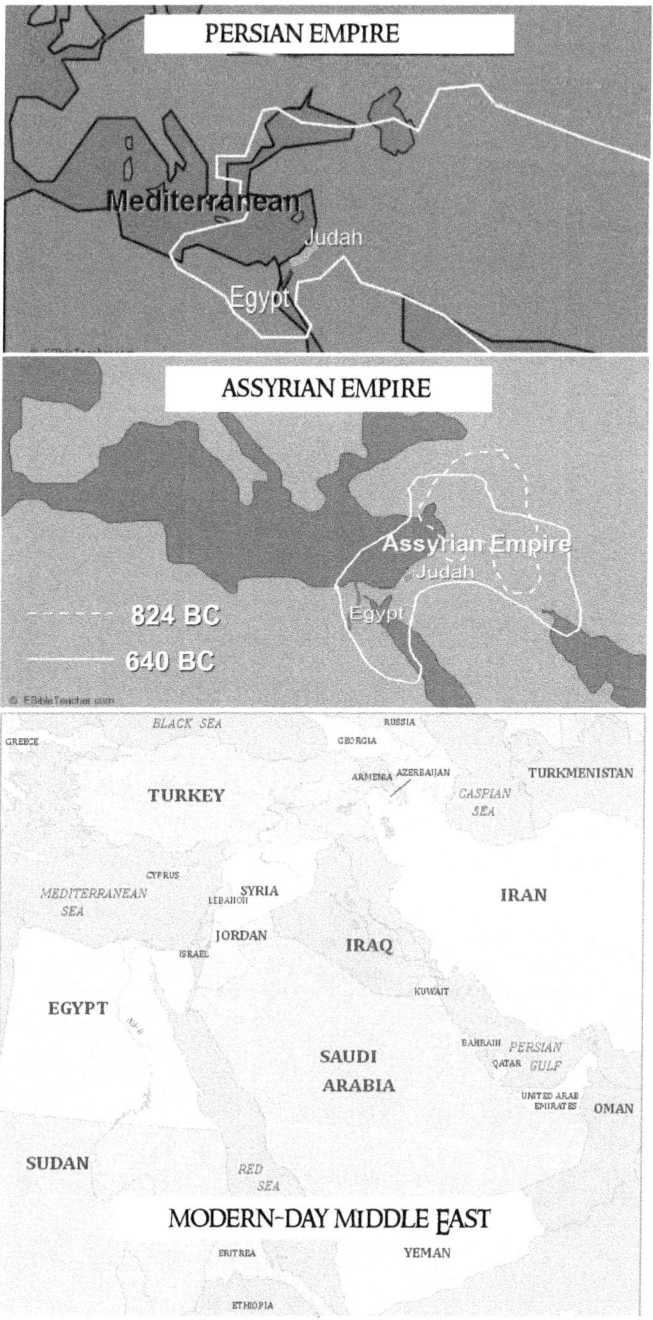
PERSIAN EMPIRE
Mediterranean
Judah
Egypt
ASSYRIAN EMPIRE
Assyrian Empire
Judah
Egypt
824 BC
640 BC
© EBibleTeacher.com
BLACK SEA
RUSSIA
GREECE
GEORGIA
ARMENIA
AZERBAIJAN
TURKMENISTAN
TURKEY
CASPIAN SEA
CYPRUS
MEDITERRANEAN SEA
SYRIA
LEBANON
IRAN
JORDAN
IRAQ
ISRAEL
KUWAIT
EGYPT
BAHRAIN
PERSIAN GULF
QATAR
SAUDI ARABIA
UNITED ARAB EMIRATES
OMAN
SUDAN
RED SEA
MODERN-DAY MIDDLE EAST
ERITREA
YEMEN
ETHIOPIA

ASSYRIAN & BABYLONIAN KINGDOMS
9TH TO 6TH CENTURIES B.C.

Assyrian Kingdom about 824 B.C.
Assyrian Kingdom about 640 B.C.
Babylonian Kingdom about 550 B.C.

Major Powers 670-550 B.C.
Kingdom of Lydia 670-546 B.C.
Kingdom of the Medes 612-550 B.C.
Babylonian Kingdom 550 B.C.
(Dan. 2&7)
Kingdom of Egypt 663-525 B.C.

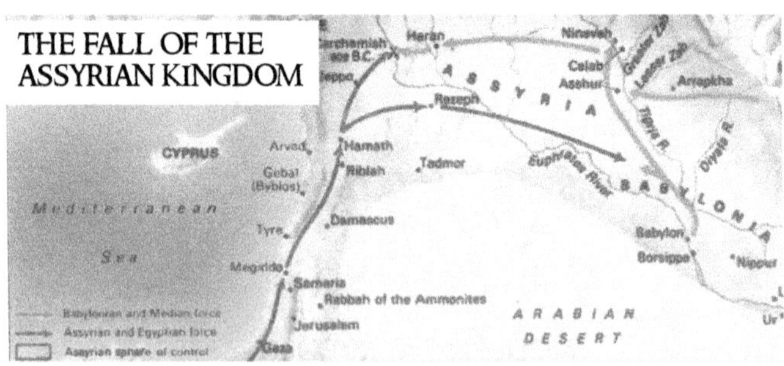

THE CONQUESTS OF ALEXANDER THE GREAT

ABOUT THE 5TH CENTURY B.C.

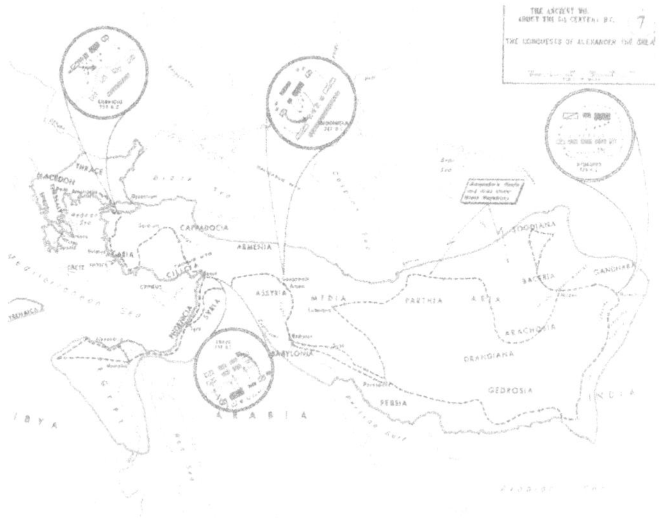

EMPIRE OF ALEXANDER THE GREAT

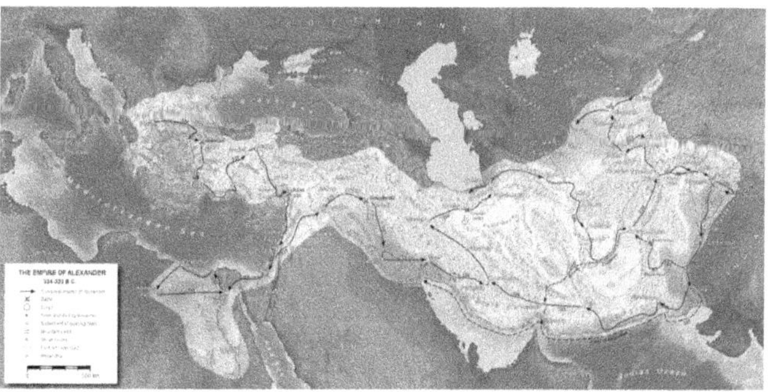

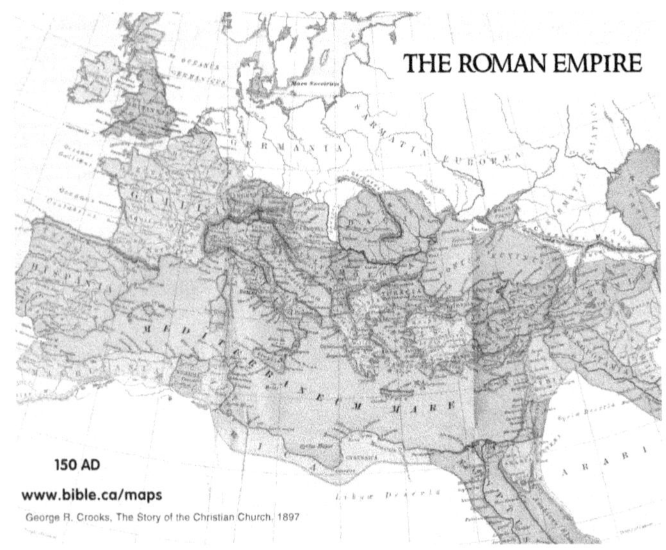

ANCIENT NEAR EASTERN WORLD

CREATION - 1570 B.C.

After the flood Nimrod, which was in Noah's line became the world's first ruler. He began in the city of Babylon (Man's City) to build the Tower of Babel until God put a stop to it. In the Fullness of Time the antichrist will claim to be the world's last ruler, until Christ comes to start his 1,000 year reign in Jerusalem (God's City). At that time Christ will throw the antichrist and the false prophet alive into the lake of fire.

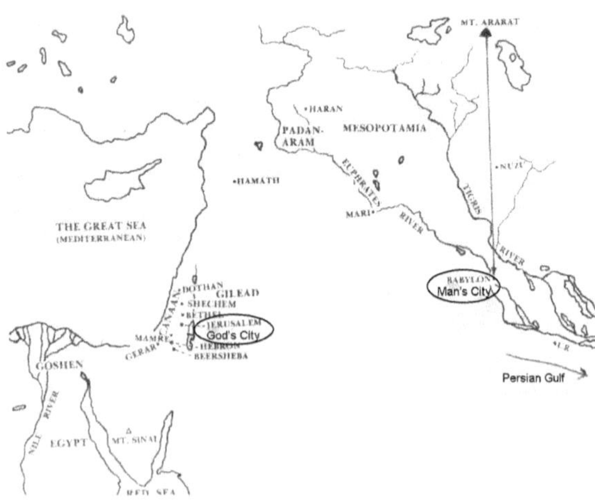

www.ingramcontent.com/pod-product-compliance
Lightning Source LLC
LaVergne TN
LVHW020632100826
845148LV00012B/2144